Food Restraint and Fasting in
Victorian Religion and Literature

NEW DIRECTIONS IN RELIGION AND LITERATURE

This series aims to showcase new work at the forefront of religion and literature through short studies written by leading and rising scholars in the field. Books will pursue a variety of theoretical approaches as they engage with writing from different religious and literary traditions. Collectively, the series will offer a timely critical intervention to the interdisciplinary crossover between religion and literature, speaking to wider contemporary interests and mapping out new directions for the field in the early twenty-first century.

Series editors: Emma Mason and Mark Knight

ALSO AVAILABLE IN THE SERIES:

The New Atheist Novel, Arthur Bradley and Andrew Tate
Blake. Wordsworth. Religion, Jonathan Roberts
Do the Gods Wear Capes?, Ben Saunders
England's Secular Scripture, Jo Carruthers
Victorian Parables, Susan E. Colón
The Late Walter Benjamin, John Schad
Dante and the Sense of Transgression, William Franke
The Glyph and the Gramophone, Luke Ferretter
John Cage and Buddhist Ecopoetics, Peter Jaeger
Rewriting the Old Testament in Anglo-Saxon Verse, Samantha Zacher
Forgiveness in Victorian Literature, Richard Hughes Gibson
The Gospel According to the Novelist, Magdalena Mączyńska
Jewish Feeling, Richa Dwor
Beyond the Willing Suspension of Disbelief, Michael Tomko
The Gospel According to David Foster Wallace, Adam S. Miller
Pentecostal Modernism, Stephen Shapiro and Philip Barnard
The Bible in the American Short Story, Lesleigh Cushing Stahlberg and Peter S. Hawkins
Faith in Poetry, Michael D. Hurley
Jeanette Winterson and Religion, Emily McAvan
Religion and American Literature since the 1950s, Mark Eaton
Esoteric Islam in Modern French Thought, Ziad Elmarsafy
The Rhetoric of Conversion in English Puritan Writing, David Parry
Djuna Barnes and Theology, Zhao Ng

FORTHCOMING:

Christian Heresy, James Joyce and the Modernist Literary Imagination, Gregory Erikson
Marilynne Robinson's Wordly Gospel, Ryan S. Kemp and Jordan M. Rodgers
Weird Faith in 19th Century Literature, Mark Knight and Emma Mason
The Economy of Religion in American Literature, Andrew Ball

Food Restraint and Fasting in Victorian Religion and Literature

Lesa Scholl

BLOOMSBURY ACADEMIC
LONDON • NEW YORK • OXFORD • NEW DELHI • SYDNEY

BLOOMSBURY ACADEMIC
Bloomsbury Publishing Plc
50 Bedford Square, London, WC1B 3DP, UK
1385 Broadway, New York, NY 10018, USA
29 Earlsfort Terrace, Dublin 2, Ireland

BLOOMSBURY, BLOOMSBURY ACADEMIC and the Diana logo
are trademarks of Bloomsbury Publishing Plc

First published in Great Britain 2022
This paperback edition published 2023

Copyright © Lesa Scholl, 2022

Lesa Scholl has asserted her right under the Copyright, Designs
and Patents Act, 1988, to be identified as Author of this work.

For legal purposes the Acknowledgements on pp. ix–x constitute
an extension of this copyright page.

Cover design: Eleanor Rose
Cover image © EVGENII ZINOVEV/ Alamy Stock Photo

All rights reserved. No part of this publication may be reproduced or transmitted in any form or by any means, electronic or mechanical, including photocopying, recording, or any information storage or retrieval system, without prior permission in writing from the publishers.

Bloomsbury Publishing Plc does not have any control over, or responsibility for, any third-party websites referred to or in this book. All internet addresses given in this book were correct at the time of going to press. The author and publisher regret any inconvenience caused if addresses have changed or sites have ceased to exist, but can accept no responsibility for any such changes.

A catalogue record for this book is available from the British Library.

A catalog record for this book is available from the Library of Congress.

ISBN: HB: 978-1-3502-5651-4
PB: 978-1-3502-5655-2
ePDF: 978-1-3502-5652-1
eBook: 978-1-3502-5653-8

Series: New Directions in Religion and Literature

Typeset by Integra Software Services Pvt. Ltd.

To find out more about our authors and books visit www.bloomsbury.com
and sign up for our newsletters.

For M, my C & E

Contents

Acknowledgements		ix
Introduction: Ethical food restraint – choosing moderation		1
Anglicanism and anorexia		8
Self-moderation and social justice		15
1	Elizabeth Gaskell, ethical economics and ethical eating	23
	Dietary abstinence and social empathy	25
	'Elegant economy' and mutual restraint	33
	Purposeful shared eating and hospitality	39
2	Christina Rossetti, spiritual growth and social justice	47
	Rossetti's materialist theology and fasting	48
	Unity of the body	55
	Liturgical practice	59
	Social prophecy	66
3	Josephine Butler's hagiography as social prophecy	77
	The social and political influence of a saint	80
	Catharine of Siena's anorexic space	89
	Britain's gluttonous capitalism	98
	Duty of the heart and body	102
4	Alice Meynell's fasting and the health of the body	109
	Meynell's fasting and dietary restraint	113
	Poetry as theology of the body	119
	Defence of the Catholic social mission	126

Conclusion: One body	133
Public health and the Body of Christ	135
Self-moderation and the health of the nation	136
Bibliography	141
Index	151

Acknowledgements

This work could not have been completed without the generous three-month fellowship I had at the Armstrong Browning Library at Baylor University. The faith and support that Josh King and Jennifer Borderud have shown in my research vision has been beyond encouraging, and I'm grateful for the opportunity they gave me to spend that semester at Baylor. Apart from the extraordinary archives, it was the extraordinary people and wealth of knowledge that I encountered made that time so significant. I'm indebted to the amazing Christi Klempnauer, Laura French and Melvin Schuetz at the ABL, and the incredible humanities research librarian, Eileen Bentsen. There are so many people at Baylor who not only made me feel at home, but also taught me much, including Kevin Gardner, Deirdre Fulton, Natalie Carnes, Joe Stubenrauch, Katie Calloway, Mona Choucair, Julia Daniels, Lauren Barron and Kristen Pond. I was also able to reconnect with fellow visiting scholars, Susan Oliver and Jonathan White, whose friendship and support means so much. I also need to thank my staff and college council at Kathleen Lumley College for allowing me the time to take up the fellowship, and my students for their gracious feedback on my research when I presented to them what I had been working on that kept me in another hemisphere.

The Gaskell Society of Japan invited me to speak at their 30th Anniversary AGM at Waseda University. Their hospitality was beyond compare, especially that of Noriko Matsunaga, Akiko Kimura and Kazuko Uda. It was a privilege to share my early work on this project with you, and to learn from you. In Adelaide, I've received much support from Jennie Shaw, Jennifer Clark, Katie Barclay, Rachel Ankeny and the Food Values Research Group. I'm grateful to my AVSA colleagues, Mandy Treagus, Michelle Smith and Madeleine

Seys. At the University of Exeter, Regenia Gagnier, Ayesha Mukherjee, Christopher Stokes, Kate Hext, Tricia Zakreski and Corinna Wagner. Also in the UK, Andy Tate, Jo Carruthers, the 'Pink Ladies', Lizzie Ludlow, Brian Murray and Matt Ingleby. You've given me opportunities to share my research, but most importantly, I value the friendships we've formed. In North America, I have too many generous and kind colleagues to mention, across the BWWA, NAVSA and MVSA. But mention must be made of my dear soul sister, Heidi Hakimi-Hood, the unflappable Emily Morris and Wendy Williams. Linda Hughes's belief in my work has sent me on a number of academic journeys that I never would have imagined. Her kindness, generosity, integrity and sense of justice continue to model for me the scholar I dream of being.

Emma Mason and Mark Knight have encouraged this project and I am thankful for their support and feedback. At Bloomsbury, Ben Doyle and Laura Cope have been superb. Susan Isaac at the Royal College of Surgeons Library helped me enormously in some archival detective work, as did Hanna Clutterbuck-Cook at the Medical Heritage Library and Louisa Yates at Gladstone's Library, while Eleanor Mackenzie and the team at Liverpool Special Collections helped me to access rare Josephine Butler materials.

My parents continue to support the fulfilment of every crazy dream I have, including the recent most special one: my precious Baylor-pup, named for the university that was so transformative for me, has been my greatest joy and love. I'm grateful for his snuggles and cheekiness, his bravery and love.

Introduction: Ethical food restraint – choosing moderation

Nothing is better calculated to remind us of the charge which is laid upon us in the exercise of our bodily functions, than the practice of fasting at stated periods, as enjoined by our Church. The frequent recurrence of the inquiry, how far our senses and appetites are under our control, is a discipline which cannot fail to produce the most wholesome effects upon both body and soul.
— [Robert Bentley Todd], *Remarks on Fasting*, 1848[1]

Food practices are fraught in modernity. Because eating is both deeply intimate and inherently social, anxieties about food centre not just on the individual body, but on the individual's relation to the world around them: what Yuki Masami refers to as 'an intense sense of interconnectedness between the human body and the environment'.[2] As Janet Chrzan suggests, food operates as a 'material marker for other cultural processes', becoming the 'item of significance' that 'delineate[s] wider cultural patterns and forces'.[3] From the medieval sumptuary laws, which regulated consumption according to social class, to twenty-first-century preoccupations with orthorexia, the visceral human need for sustenance has made food access and consumption integral to social and economic agency and responsibility. Masami highlights the difference between food as the substance we eat and meals as not just the food but the context in which we consume it as she observes that 'meals' are what shapes individuals and communities 'not only physically but also mentally', undergirding the communality and interconnectedness of eating,⁴ even in a modernity predicated on 'egoism, loneliness, isolation and social disorganization'.⁵ The consumption of food entangles the natural world. 'Since all people eat', Julia Abramson suggests, 'food and ethics should interest all people, whether as consumers or producers or both… Just as food mirrors our relationships to community and society, it also reflects our interactions with nature'. She continues, 'food and ethics addresses humans and human cultures, but also other forms of life and the environment'.⁶

Popular conversations about food restraint and health in the twenty-first century often turn on issues such as anorexia nervosa or the obesity epidemic, yet engagement with food history and ecocriticism extends food restraint into the arena of ethics, in which it becomes more about the corporal than the individual, and the place of humanity within the natural world. When ethics are brought into the frame, common social narratives revolve around themes such as vegetarianism and veganism, or, from another direction, fair trade and 'small planet' thinking.⁷ These issues are complex and intersecting, leading some scholars to question 'whether or not ethical consumption is a field that is simply too large and fractured to be meaningful'.⁸ Rachel Ankeny similarly notes that even defining what is meant by 'ethical consumerism' is 'a vexed issue', with attempts 'to make ethical food decisions' resulting in 'contradictory outcomes', and furthermore it 'cannot be described in terms of a set of shared values, beliefs, or politics on the part of its practitioners'. Ankeny emphasizes the personal in ethical consumption in facilitating ethical consumption as 'a set of diverse and often conflicting food choices that are voluntary and outwardly directed as a result of the actor's beliefs about his or her values [and] responsibilities'.⁹ Ethics become simultaneously deeply personal while necessarily outward-focused.

Tania Lewis and Emily Potter describe this internal contradiction as 'ordinary ethics', in which the notion of 'ethical' is 'not necessarily tied to a stable external moral framework but rather speaks to what is at once a more pluralized and privatized moral universe.[10] Indeed, this description reflects the move that occurred during the timeframe of this study, from the externalized moral economy of the late eighteenth century to the more individualized ideas of ethical consumption in the nineteenth century, which can be seen as a result of capitalism or, alternatively, a move toward an internalized ethical approach that Zygmunt Bauman refers to as 'planetary responsibility'.[11] Bauman's planetary responsibility is founded on absolute interdependence: the

> acknowledgment of the fact that all of us who share the planet depend on one another for our present and our future, that nothing we do or fail to do is indifferent to the fate of anybody else, and that no longer can any of us seek and find private shelter from storms that originate in any part of the globe.[12]

Within this extreme interdependence, Bauman observes the key problem of individualized or 'ordinary' ethics: 'Once shifted over (or abandoned) to individuals, the task of ethical decision making becomes overwhelming, as the stratagem of hiding behind a recognized and apparently indomitable authority... is no longer a viable or reliable option'. While emphasizing the individual's 'unconditional responsibility', Bauman also recognizes that '[s]truggling with so daunting a task casts the actors into a state of permanent uncertainty' in the face of 'mind-boggling complexity' instead of an externalized list of 'must-do and mustn't-do rules'.[13] In spite of the complexities, however, he asserts the human responsibility to grapple with these challenges. Within the space of food consumption, rather than seeking right or wrong moral (externally defined) definitions, grappling in such a way means to work within the internal tensions and contradictions to develop ethical foodscapes.

In defining the scope of ethical foodscapes, Michael K. Goodman, Damian Maye and Lewis Holloway state:

Food ethics are about performances – affective, moral, material – of when 'bodies meet' foods... [these] are relational ethics, the experiences of which are of a very intimate kind... Food and food ethics are thus *relationally performative* as they involve the linking up of the material and constructed self with Others and Other natures in moral webs of meanings through the performances of producing, shopping, making, serving, eating, and ultimately, 'wasting'. These relational performatives of food ethics are fundamentally situated within psychological, cultural, political, social, economic, and ecological contexts, each with their own powerful moral webs of meanings and materialities created by but also shaping food ethics.[14]

The material and ideological are inherently linked in this framework, revealing the messiness of what it means to eat 'good' food, or even to eat 'well', ideas that are fundamental to this study. *Food Restraint and Fasting in Victorian Religion and Literature* combines theology, ethics, nutrition and economics to ask questions not just about *why* some Victorians showed restraint, but what constituted restraint, and what counted as excess – either overeating or undereating – from a dietary perspective. Excess and moderation are unavoidably culturally contingent, and therefore it is necessary to understand what these terms meant in Victorian Britain, particularly given the issues of famine and widespread poverty alongside the rise of consumerism and capitalist political economy as essential elements of Britain's imperial structure. Most crucially, however, this study focuses on historical, theological and literary examples of restraining food consumption out of a consciousness of one's own prosperity in comparison to the scarcity of others, and out of a desire to give what one would have otherwise consumed or wasted to those in need – an individualized, 'ordinary' ethics. While the respective social visions may be derived from theological and therefore moral and external motivations, I argue that the individual decision to restrain consumption and what to do out of that restraint is deeply personal and ethical, tied to an internal conviction in which there was no delineation between belief and action: morals and ethics are entangled.

With industrialization becoming entrenched in Britain through the late eighteenth and nineteenth centuries, the changing economic structures and philosophies inevitably altered social structures and practices. Poverty was not new, nor was hunger; but they were focalized in a new way, perhaps most dramatically through the passing of the New Poor Law in 1834. The previous Poor Law had received years of criticism due to its inefficacy; however, the new law was, as has been most eloquently argued by E. P. Thompson, 'the most sustained attempt to impose an ideological dogma, in defiance of the evidence of human need, in English history'.[5] Yet this was also an historical moment in which social power and social voice gained momentum. While concepts such as political economy's distribution of wealth were articulated and, often, bastardized to justify inhumane social and political policies, they also gave access to concepts unavailable in a feudal mindset. For example, ideas of 'collective responsibility' led to the rise of friendly societies which, Penelope Ismay argues, 'comprised the largest social movement of the age and provided significant financial security for millions of working-class households'.[6] In 'Consumer-Owned Community Flour and Bread Societies' (1998), Joshua Bamfield discusses the emergence of cooperatives in the wake of the late eighteenth-century Flour Wars. The examples of communities working together to make staples accessible to as many people as possible were forerunners of the trade unions of the nineteenth century. Another key example is found in Kathryn Gleadle's work on Katherine Plymley's diaries. Plymley's brother, the Archdeacon of Salop, was at the forefront of developing dietary restriction societies during the late eighteenth and early nineteenth centuries. These societies, along with the trade union and cooperative movements, were initially formed from a motive of ethical compassion for others within the community to counteract the increasing disparity between wealth and poverty. As Amartya Sen points out in *Poverty and Famines* (2003),

> Starvation is the characteristic of some people not *having* enough food to eat. It is not the characteristic of there not *being* enough to eat... Leaving out cases in which a person may deliberately starve, starvation statements translate readily into statements of ownership of food by persons.[17]

Ethical food restraint is an act that at its core seeks to readdress the imbalance of food ownership. It requires the one who fasts or restrains to recognize the institutionally entrenched social structure of privilege and disadvantage, acknowledge their own privilege and be willing to contend with it.

A significant yet under-researched way that individuals were encouraged to contend with their own privilege in newly industrialized, commodified, nineteenth-century Britain was through a food restraint that considered consumption in general: questions over what is necessary and what is superfluous, overlaid with a moral and ethical consciousness that recognized the abject poverty of others within their own community. Individuals were provoked to acknowledge the visibility of the poor and their own power to do something – even something small – to help. Parallel to that provocation was to ask oneself how one can live with integrity alongside such visibility – how does one reconcile going to assist in an impoverished hovel, and then returning home to an eight-course meal? In their introduction to *Economic Women* (2013), Lana Dalley and Jill Rappoport note that the New Poor Law of 1834 was a turning point in economic and community thought, away from ideas of 'community care' and 'traditional ideas of a parish's responsibility' for the poor, toward 'less personal notions of independent contract and self-help'.[18] They also observe, importantly, that these boundaries are never as clear-cut in practice. Indeed, central to my project is to argue that the social movements for dietary reform that Gleadle writes of as preceding the New Poor Law persisted throughout the nineteenth century, although perhaps less visible because they were less institutionalized.

Alongside the rise of industrialization, the late eighteenth century experienced some particularly bad harvests due to weather events such as hurricanes, which led to significant economic precarity and social unrest. Gleadle notes the number of 'subscription societies and projects of dietary reform (such as abstaining from the consumption of wheat and corn to preserve them for the poor)' which arose during this time.[19] These projects existed in parallel to other movements like the sugar boycott; however, unlike the sugar boycott, which was a protest for the sake of ending the slavery from which the privileged benefitted, these dietary reform projects were focused much closer to home and were intended to have a much more direct impact on economic disparities. That is, the privileged restricted what they ate, and what they would have otherwise eaten or thrown away was then made available to the poor in the same community. Katherine Plymley's brother, while participating in dietary reform, wrote recipes for the *Shrewsbury Chronicle* suggesting alternative ways of eating – such as bread made with potato rather than wheat – and articles encouraging the consumption of brown wheat rather than refined, as well as the restriction of eating bread only at breakfast instead of at every meal so that distribution could be more equitable.[20] These community-based movements had a broader national impact. Gleadle writes of the privy council and both houses of Parliament in 1795 issuing 'pledges committing themselves to dietary abstinence; [and] a Home Office circular exhorting people to attempt to reduce their consumption of wheat by a third'.[21] A similar circular was released in 1801.[22] This kind of social movement was quite prominent in Britain's social history and was a significant part of Victorian Britain's understanding of social justice.

Anglicanism and anorexia

Anglicanism and its nineteenth-century revivals through the Oxford Movement (also called the Tractarian Movement), ritualism and Anglo-Catholicism were crucial to the development of ordinary ethics and social justice in Victorian Britain, from its practical theology, its emphasis on reserve, and its renewed emphasis on the sacredness of the natural world. The Oxford Movement initiated this series of revivals through its attentiveness to Church Fathers and ritualistic devotional practices, such as fasting and the Eucharist. These practices undergird the Anglican understanding of consumption and the way in which eating or not eating reinforces the interconnectedness, not just of human society, but of all of nature. Their emphasis on the Real Presence of Christ in the Eucharistic elements, as noted by Emma Mason, reinforced 'the implication that inanimate objects like bread and wine had an invisible reality [that] confirmed [their] sense that all things, material and immaterial, are equal in God'.[23] Such ideas of equality demand an ethical response to the use and abuse enacted through consumption.

There are four women whose work I am using in this study: Elizabeth Gaskell, Christina Rossetti, Josephine Butler and Alice Meynell, each of whom were directly engaged in social justice in their lives as well as their writing and were, to varying degrees, influenced by Anglicanism and its approach to food restraint and fasting. The influence of Anglicanism is central to this study, primarily because of the religion's systematized approach toward fasting, which was adopted with variations across a broad range of socially engaged people. The way in which the Tractarian Movement's social vision entwined with their theology also made its tenets of individual responsibility within one's community attractive from an ethical perspective.[24] Elizabeth Ludlow argues that 'the main characteristic of the Tractarian approach to theology is that it is "practical" rather than speculative... For them, there is no distinction between theology and spirituality'.[25] This embodied theology goes beyond the metaphysical understanding of an 'intimate connection between the seemingly intangible content of faith and the physical forms through which it is revealed in the world meant that everything was a type and therefore sacred' to an imperative as to how to act in response to that understanding.[26] Mason suggests that 'Anglo-Catholics... believed that because God was revealed analogically through nature, it was the Christian's responsibility to engage with the world as an interconnected and social union',[27] and indeed it is the incarnational theology of Anglicanism that undergirded their social vision that valued the inherent equality of all humans. Writing specifically of Rossetti's theology, Mason extends this understanding to all of the natural world:

> The incarnational nature of God's being in Jesus was a constant reminder to Rossetti that all of creation is made of the divine and so interdependent with itself. Rossetti's Jesus was not only God made flesh, but God made into all things, a composite of multiple species, beings, and substances.[28]

She further explains,

> As a movement that saw nature as a codified revelation of the Trinity, Tractarianism directed the believer to the things of the world, human, floral, animal, mineral, as part of a network in which every being was connected with the divine. It also urged Christians to consider it their duty to remain vigilant in ensuring these connections remained unbroken, especially when confronted with... the 'signs of the times' – natural disasters, war, climate change, and industrialism.[29]

Mason's understanding of Rossetti's theology reveals the motives of Anglicanism to focus on the responsibility of humanity both to recognize the sacredness of the earth (as opposed to human dominion of it) and to care for that earth as a form of holy worship. While my study is more primarily attending to intra-human relationships, the broader ecological understanding of the sacredness of nature remains important because of the impact of the 'signs of the times' on human vulnerability. By recognizing the interconnectedness of all things in the divine, the ethical shift toward active compassion and self-reflection regarding consumption becomes imperative. Within the structures of Anglicanism, there is a blending between the moral (external) and ethical (internal) convictions that drives the mode of social action I address.

A part of my argument is that the fasts and feasts of the Anglican liturgical calendar operated to moderate fasting – to prevent it from becoming excessive, with excess being indicative of self-focus, whereas moderation enables an outward focus. In Tract 18 of *Tracts for the Times, Thoughts on the Benefits of the System of Fasting* (1833), Edward Pusey suggests that while the 'external restraint' of the liturgical calendar might seem to hinder private judgement, it both moderates zeal and reinforces the fact that 'although religion is in one sense strictly individual, yet in the means by which it is kept alive, it is essentially expansive and social'.[30] Fasting, then, is not merely about the individual faster's spiritual growth, but a communal act, performed corporately. The reasons for this are practical. It is to resist the drive of consumerism, luxury and excess inherent in liberal capitalism; but it is also so that through the moderation of those who *have* that provision is made for those who have *not*. Quoting Augustine, Pusey writes: 'A true Fast is not merely to keep under the body, but to give to the widow, or the poor, the amount of that which thou wouldest have expended upon thyself'.[31] The emphasis of fasting in this sense is very much community-based and ethical, not merely individual and spiritual. It has a horizontal vision outward to the community, not just vertical up to the divine. In its dual upward and outward focus, fasting is also meant as a form of social prophecy to bring conviction to those given to selfishness, gluttony and excess.

Pusey's perspective on fasting intervenes in a cultural and historical moment in which two extremes of food restraint occur, both of which are gendered. There were famous cases in the nineteenth century of 'fasting girls' – mostly children but some young women – who, like the medieval saints, claimed divine strength to resist food and drink. This kind of food restraint is known as anorexia mirabilis, or the miraculous ability not to eat. It was also in this period that anorexia nervosa became pathologized as a psychological disorder; and understandably anorexia mirabilis and anorexia nervosa were often blurred, with debate and division rising between theology and medicine. Pusey's model of fasting differs from both types of anorexia, for it not only resists gendering, but because its focus involves caring for the poor, one who fasts must do so in a way that avoids drawing attention to oneself while enabling the physical and mental strength to do the work of looking after others, rather than fasters themselves becoming incapacitated and lethargic through hunger

A great deal of scholarship has been done on women and the anorexic body in the nineteenth century, key works being, among others, Leslie Heywood's *Dedication to Hunger: The Anorexic Aesthetic in Modern Culture* (1996) and Anna Krugovoy Silver's *Victorian Literature and the Anorexic Body* (2002).[32] Both studies are relevant to *Food Restraint and Fasting* in the way they address anorexia nervosa and anorexia mirabilis. Heywood questions the divisions between the two types of food refusal, whereas Silver draws a firmer line; however, both types of anorexia are problematic in that they remove agency from the person fasting. They are predicated in terms of being out of control – whether due to divine intervention or to psychological disorder – and of excessive, irrational behaviour. The language of excess is itself gendered, despite the many male fasters who, because of their extreme abstinence (both sexual and alimentary), were cast as effeminate. Many of them converted to Roman Catholicism, in itself seen as an extreme, where fasting was perceived as punishing and diminishing the carnal flesh. It did not assist the Anglican cause that key figures in the Oxford Movement, like John Henry Newman and Gerard Manley Hopkins, converted to Rome. Fasting in the Anglican context, however, was much more akin to Eastern Orthodox fasting in which portions were restricted rather than abstaining from whole meals. Yes, fasting was about disciplining the body, but not punishing it. It was about creating a sense of awareness within the body, which, arguably, would increase agency rather than diminish it. In 'The Science and Spirituality of Nutrition' (1999), John Coveney argues that 'a dietary asceticism that problematizes the body… is directly related to the Christian notion of ethics', suggesting that such practices lend individuals the capacity to know themselves 'as ethical subjects'.[33] He cites Foucault's understanding of self-surveillance as a part of governmentality, connecting such understanding to the 'self-discipline and training' of what Foucault calls 'technologies of the self': the 'techniques' one uses 'to know and act on themselves'.[34] Importantly in the Anglican context, this discipline was given a practical and socially focused purpose: ideologically it was a protest against the broader selfishness of a capitalist society and therefore part of a broader vision of social justice and ethical consumption. There was a rationality and order to this kind of fasting, reinforced through the liturgical calendar, which asserts an agency in fasting that the frameworks of anorexia mirabilis and anorexia nervosa diminish.

It may seem that the kind of food restraint or fasting that this study addresses has little to do with either type of anorexia; yet the problem is that in practice, motivations bleed across each other. As a case in point, to recall the Plymley family, the Archdeacon's daughter Jane began, out of an ethical consciousness, to eat only the food that was available to the poor in their community. She chose to resist her own privilege. However, this resistance led to her refusing to eat with her family as she ate less and less. Jane Plymley died of starvation at the age of twenty. What began as a rational choice became as excessive and out of control as it was tragic. Yet even with such cases there is scope for a triangulation of motivation that allows for a type of food restraint that involves rational choice, rather than something entirely out of the faster's control. I deliberately use the term 'food restraint' rather than 'food refusal' to express a space for agency. However, it is important to understand the culture of nutrition in order to determine what is *excessive* fasting: it is necessary to establish what is considered enough food in the first place.

Fasting was contentious within Anglicanism. Robert Wilson Evans, a clergyman, was sceptical of extreme fasting.[35] In *Ministry of the Body* (1847) he argues that those who fast seek to remove themselves not just from their own bodies, but from the social body which was in opposition to their Christian duty: 'We think to go by pure abstract spirit, and so far to neglect the province of the body, that we find some actually laying it down as a rule, that the further they go from the bodily, the nearer they come to the spiritual'.[36] This abstraction is, in Evans's view, an abdication of true spiritual responsibility and achieves nothing: 'When we have denied in any way the body, do we in so much necessarily advance into the spirit? when we starve the body, do we feed the spirit? when we humble the body, do we exalt the spirit?'[37]

In essence, Evans aligns with the Oxford Movement's attitude that the natural progression from individual spiritual growth is to active social work in the community; yet in extreme fasting, where one locks oneself away to fast, they are failing to be the Church which 'is, at the very least, a body of men linked by bonds of visible action'.[38] Evans sees a hypocrisy in fasting without action, 'much in the same way as they held charity who were content to say, "Depart in peace; be ye warmed and filled." It wants growth from want of exercise on its proper outward objects'.[39] Evans's criticism of fasting, however, was refuted a year later by Robert Bentley Todd, an eminent physician and surgeon who was a part of John Henry Newman's inner circle at Oxford. He was a prolific contributor to the body of medical knowledge that emerged from the nineteenth century and was known to be critical of faddish and extreme dieting. *Remarks on Fasting* (1848) was published anonymously, perhaps because Newman's conversion to Roman Catholicism two years earlier would have sullied the public reception of Todd's defence of fasting. His perspective is, however, consistent with that which Pusey expressed in his tracts on fasting for *Tracts for the Times*, and thus very much in line with Anglicanism.

Todd acknowledges that 'ill-directed fasting' can be dangerous, 'especially if at other times diet be not carefully regulated', and admits that it has 'done serious harm to many persons of delicate constitution'.[40] However, he also emphasizes that for the most part society is given to gluttony and could therefore benefit physically as well as spiritually by proper fasting – something that he, as the physician, offers to teach Evans so that the clergyman can teach his flock. He agrees with Evans on the importance of caring for the body because of its intimate association with the soul and says that 'the slightest disturbance in the former [the body] exercises the most potent influence (often insensibly) over the latter; and that the complexion of our thoughts and feelings takes its hue chiefly from the habitual condition or temperament of our body'.[41] Thus a habit of *moderate* fasting is a healthful practice. Moderation is key. Todd acknowledges that fasting 'indiscreetly practised, carried too far' can 'induce habits of indolence instead of energy, bring on a state of nervous irritability, weaken the powers of the intellect, and so impair the exercise of the will'.[42] However, while making this admission, he also points out that gluttony is a much greater risk in his society than excessive starvation:

> The generality of persons are apt to err on the side of excess, and not only do they take too much, but they eat too quickly... To such persons, the observance of the Church's fasts must prove extremely beneficial, if for nothing else, at least for their bodily health. The

weekly fasts on Fridays, and on the other days appointed by the Church, not only gives rest to their digestive organs, but it may also wean them from many bad customs in their habitual mode of living.[43]

Self-moderation and social justice

In *Bourgeois Consumption* (2011), Rachel Rich argues

> The tensions between ideals and practices among bourgeois men and women can be characterised as the struggle between gluttony and moderation. In their eating habits, the bourgeoisie lived out these opposing tensions, which at their most extreme could be seen through the emergence of an obsession with digestive disorders, and the discovery of anorexia nervosa. The eating habits of the bourgeoisie are, therefore, a useful path for discovering the tensions around which bourgeois identity and experience were continually renegotiated.[44]

This tension is a necessary counterpoint to those figures who deliberately showed restraint in consumption in order to resist the excessive consumerism they saw in their society. The ethical food restraint addressed in *Food Restraint and Fasting* is motivated by an ambivalence toward, if not disgust for, the kind of excess that leads to waste in light of the poverty that persisted in Britain. Pusey's tracts on fasting position the practice in terms of rationality and order in a world that is chaotically out of control in its pursuit of excess. In a world where excess and selfishness are worshipped, moderation is reconceived as irrational; it is such a culture that would question why one would show restraint in the first place, rather than why one would consume more than the body physically requires. As Silver notes, the Anglican attitude toward food was that people 'must eat because the body requires food, but they should eat only as much as their health demands, not merely for pleasure'.⁴⁵ Yet in the cultural context of food consumption, diet is rarely solely to do with nutritional requirements. Sen tellingly writes:

> [T]he translation of minimum *nutritional* requirements into minimum *food* requirements depends of the choice of commodities… Typically, it turns out to be very low-cost indeed, but monumentally boring, and people's food habits are not, in fact, determined by such a cost minimization exercise. The actual incomes at which specified nutritional requirements are met will depend greatly on the consumption habits of the people in question.⁴⁶

Most importantly, Sen argues that food choices, and commodity choices in general, speak to the consumer's social and economic agency, the 'legitimacy' of their ownership within structures of entitlement. In addressing poverty, Sen argues for a move away from 'thinking in terms of what *exists*' to thinking 'in terms of who can *command* what': that is, who has the privilege of choice.⁴⁷

This concept of privilege and agency closely relates to ethical food restraint. In a society that is predicated on a fear of loss,⁴⁸ the tendency is to hoard for oneself; it therefore requires a sense of security – whether in one's economic status or in divine provision – to have the willingness to sacrifice some of that privilege by moderating one's consumption. In *Otherwise Than Being* (1981), Emmanuel Levinas argues, however, that one is not truly human until one takes the bread out of one's own mouth to give it to the other.⁴⁹ Humanity is thus predicated on a willingness to sacrifice: not just giving out of one's excess, but in giving at pains to oneself. Giving, in Levinas's view, requires the giver to know what it is, in terms of pleasure or enjoyment, that they are giving up. This then extends to the concept of fasting, not just in terms of giving food, but in being willing to sacrifice one's social and economic privilege. In a similar vein, Pusey writes, 'Only let us not mock GOD, let us deny ourselves in something which is to us really self-denial; let us, in whatever degree we may be able to bear it without diminishing our own usefulness, put ourselves to some inconvenience'.[50] He expresses the necessity of self-sacrifice – the putting oneself to pains – but, importantly, this is moderated by not going to an extreme that would debilitate the one who fasts. In this way, Pusey sets up fasting against the representation of the apparently divinely inspired fasting girls, some of whom starved to death, others revealed as frauds. Rather than becoming a kind of spectacle, or damaging one's health, regular and regulated fasting should be done privately with an outward, practical purpose.

Each of the four chapters of *Food Restraint and Fasting* takes an element of Pusey's approach to fasting as its trellis, although these elements are necessarily and intricately connected. By focusing on Elizabeth Gaskell's novels, the first chapter foregrounds this study with the complexities of eating and not eating within a community context. Gaskell uses her novels to create empathy for the poor and vulnerable, but also reveals how such empathy is often conflicted when brought into practice through food restraint. Gaskell's emphasis on community feeling ties in with Christina Rossetti's concept of fellow-feeling, which underpins her materialist theology. The second chapter examines Rossetti's theological writing relating to fasting and the way in which it is intended to create fellow-feeling and unity in the Body of Christ, as well as to inspire and enable active social intervention. Rossetti's theological work is also considered in terms of social prophecy and is therefore usefully followed by the chapter on Josephine Butler, who represents fasting in her hagiographic work to enact her social prophecy. The final chapter examines food restraint and physical health through the complex figure of Alice Meynell. Meynell embodies all the motivations of fasting, from the dietary fads she experimented with to improve her health as a child and adolescent, to her disengagement with food due to her dental problems, as well as her explicit abstemiousness in family meals in order to give what was left to charity. Her attitude toward food restraint was both spiritual and practical, which is evident in her famously recognized reserved writing aesthetic.

In line with David Jasper's argument regarding what he calls 'intradisciplinarity', in examining literary texts, I am not looking for 'theology or religion… lurking in disguise',[51] but rather recognizing that theology is expressed beyond what is considered conventional theological writing. This is especially true for the women I address, who were largely (although not entirely, particularly in regard to Rossetti and Butler) excluded from such genres. Rather than theology seemingly accidentally finding its way into their texts, indirectly through influence and cultural context, I would argue that they are all engaging with practical theology – whether through exegesis, parable or hagiography – and for each of these women this theology has a material purpose to encourage an active, outwardly focused attitude toward ethical food restraint for the purpose of giving to the vulnerable. Even for the Unitarian Gaskell, there was a widespread influence of millennialism that, even if they did not actually believe in the idea of Christ himself returning to the earth, they did believe in the responsibility of the Body of Christ to be a part of enacting the kingdom of heaven in the world. Writing specifically of Gaskell, Elizabeth Ludlow refers to 'the convergence of spiritual and temporal equality' in social terms, as well as the influence of F. D. Maurice's friendship – Maurice, a Broad Church theologian, becoming one of the founders of Christian Socialism.[52] The idea of seeing the kingdom of heaven on earth resonates with the vision of each of these women to a 'shared commitment to social justice and change' that would lead to a 'transformation of this world'.[53] Furthermore, the collapse of the space between the spiritual and temporal lends itself to an appreciation of the sacredness in the everyday that ties the theological understanding of aliment held by these Victorian women not just to Anglican attitudes toward consumption, but contemporary eco-theology.[54] There are current theological studies on food and excess, wrapped up in the so-called obesity epidemic of the twenty-first century, that are concerned with moderation and excess, that overlay one's engagement with food with a spiritual or divine authority. *Food Restraint and Fasting* reveals historical precedent for these kinds of narratives in the nineteenth century. Then, just as now, there were social and medical narratives that were concerned with excess in terms of self-starvation and gluttony, but also engaging with ideas of social privilege, physical want and prosperity consciousness that exerted an ethical imperative on the ways in which individuals and communities consume.

Notes

1. [Robert Bentley Todd], *Remarks on Fasting, and on the Discipline of the Body: In a Letter to a Clergyman. By A Physician* (London: Francis & John Rivington, 1848), 4–5.
2. Yuki Masami, 'Meals in the Age of Toxic Environments' in *The Routledge Companion to the Environmental Humanities*, ed. Ursula K. Heise, Jon Christensen and Michelle Niemann, 56–63 (New York and London: Routledge, 2017), 58.
3. Janet Chrzan, 'Nutritional Anthropology', in *The Routledge International Handbook of Food Studies*, ed. Ken Albala, 48–64 (London and New York: Routledge, 2013), 48.
4. Masami, 'Meals in the Age of Toxic Environments', 56.
5. Mike Featherstone, 'Foreword', in *Ethical Consumption: A Critical Introduction*, ed. Tania Lewis and Emily Potter, xvii–xxviii (London and New York: Routledge, 2010), xvii.
6. Julia Abramson, 'Food and Ethics', in *The Routledge International Handbook of Food Studies*, ed. Ken Albala, 371–8 (London and New York: Routledge, 2013), 371.
7. Ecocriticism has become a vast interdisciplinary field of study. Key works include Jason W. Moore, *Capitalism in the Web of Life: Ecology*

and the Accumulation of Capital (London: Verso, 2015), Christopher Otter, *Diet for a Large Planet: Industrial Britain, Food Systems, and World Ecology* (Chicago: University of Chicago Press, 2020) and Bill Pritchard, Rodomiro Ortiz and Meera Shekar, eds., *The Routledge Handbook on Food and Nutrition Security* (London: Routledge, 2016).

8   Jo Littler, 'What's Wrong with Ethical Consumption?' in *Ethical Consumption: A Critical Introduction*, ed. Tania Lewis and Emily Potter, 27–39 (London and New York: Routledge, 2010), 27.

9   Rachel Ankeny, 'Food and Ethical Consumption', in *The Oxford Handbook of Food History*, ed. Jeffrey M. Pilcher, 461–80 (Oxford: Oxford University Press, 2012), 462.

10 Tania Lewis and Emily Potter, 'Introducing Ethical Consumption', in *Ethical Consumption: A Critical Introduction*, 3–24 (London and New York: Routledge, 2010), 10.

11 Zygmunt Bauman, *Does Ethics Have a Chance in a World of Consumers?* Institute for Human Sciences Vienna Lecture Series (Cambridge, MA and London: Harvard University Press, 2008), 29.

12 Ibid.

13 Ibid., 51–2.

14 Michael K. Goodman, Damian Maye and Lewis Holloway, 'Ethical Foodscapes?: Premises, Promises, and Possibilities', *Environment and Planning*, 42 (2010): 1782–96, 1784. Emphasis orig.

15 E. P. Thompson, *The Making of the English Working Class* (New York: Vintage, 1966), 295.

16 Penelope Ismay, *Trust among Strangers: Friendly Societies in Modern Britain* (Cambridge: Cambridge University Press, 2018), 2.

17 Amartya Sen, *Poverty and Famines: An Essay on Entitlement and Deprivation* (Oxford: Oxford University Press, 1981), 1.

18 Lana Dalley and Jill Rappoport, 'Introducing Economic Women', in *Economic Women: Essays on Desire and Dispossession in Nineteenth-Century British Culture*, 1–21 (Columbus: The Ohio State University Press, 2013), 4–5.

19 Kathryn Gleadle, 'Gentry, Gender, and the Moral Economy during the Revolutionary and Napoleonic Wars in Provincial England', in

Economic Women: Essays on Desire and Dispossession in Nineteenth-Century British Culture, ed. Lana Dally and Jill Rappoport, 25–40 (Columbus: The Ohio State University Press, 2013), 27.

20 Ibid., 32–3.
21 Ibid., 33.
22 For the House of Commons Reports to the House of Lords on bread and corn production and distribution, see F. William Terrington, ed., *House of Lords Sessional Papers*, vol. 2 (Dobbs Ferry NY: Oceana Publications, 1975), 1–64.
23 Emma Mason, *Christina Rossetti: Poetry, Ecology, Faith* (Oxford: Oxford University Press, 2018), 58.
24 I have discussed the connection between the Oxford Movement's theology and their social vision extensively in *Hunger, Poetry and the Oxford Movement: The Tractarian Social Vision* (London: Bloomsbury, 2020).
25 Elizabeth Ludlow, *Christina Rossetti and the Bible: Waiting with the Saints* (London: Bloomsbury, 2014), 2.
26 Mason, *Christina Rossetti*, 8.
27 Ibid., 5.
28 Ibid., 4.
29 Ibid., 35.
30 Edward B. Pusey, *Thoughts on the Benefits of the System of Fasting. Tracts for the Times*, 18 (London: Rivington, 1833), 2–3.
31 Ibid., 13–14.
32 See also Joan Jacobs Brumberg, *Fasting Girls: The History of Anorexia Nervosa* (1988; New York: Vintage Books, 2000).
33 John Coveney, 'The Science and Spirituality of Nutrition', *Critical Public Health*, 9.1 (1999): 23–37, 23.
34 Ibid., 24.
35 Rev. Robert Wilson Evans, BA, MA, BD, was Archdeacon of Westmorland. He was born in Shrewsbury in 1789, at the time when Joseph Plymley was Archdeacon of Salop. While Evans became a clergyman, his father was an MD who trained at the Edinburgh School of Medicine.
36 Robert Wilson Evans, *The Ministry of the Body* (London: Francis & John Rivington, 1847), 38.

37 Ibid.
38 Ibid., 236.
39 Ibid., 213.
40 [Robert Bentley Todd], *Remarks on Fasting*, 3.
41 Ibid., 4.
42 Ibid., 6.
43 Ibid., 12.
44 Rachel Rich, *Bourgeois Consumption: Food, Space and Identity in London and Paris, 1850–1914* (Manchester and New York: Manchester University Press, 2011), 13.
45 Anna Kyugovoy Silver, *Victorian Literature and the Anorexic Body* (Cambridge: Cambridge University Press, 2002), 139.
46 Sen, *Poverty and Famines*, 12.
47 Ibid., 1–2.
48 See Jeff Nunokawa, *The Afterlife of Property: Domestic Security and the Victorian Novel* (Princeton: Princeton University Press, 1994), 7.
49 Emmanuel Levinas, *Otherwise than Being or Beyond Essence*, trans. Alphonso Lingis (1981; Pittsburgh: Duquesne University Press, 1998), 56.
50 Pusey, *Thoughts on the Benefits of the System of Fasting*, tract 18, 22.
51 David Jasper, 'Interdisciplinarity in Impossible Times: Studying Religion through Literature and the Arts', in *Literature and Theology: New Interdisciplinary Spaces*, ed. Heather Walton, 5–18 (London: Routledge, 2011), 9.
52 Elizabeth Ludlow, 'Working-Class Methodism and Eschatological Anxiety in Elizabeth Gaskell's Fiction', *The Gaskell Journal*, 34 (2020): 25–40, 37–8.
53 Ibid., 26.
54 See Norman Wirzba, *Food and Faith: A Theology of Eating* (2nd ed. Cambridge: Cambridge University Press, 2019) and *From Nature to Creation: A Christian Vision for Understanding and Loving Our World* (Grand Rapids, MI: Baker Academic, 2015).

Elizabeth Gaskell, ethical economics and ethical eating

> *I believe it is unnecessary to press on you the consideration, that the guilt of these sordid homicides is fearfully aggravated by the fact, that the victims so thrust out unto death, have an older and a better title to needful sustentation, and essential relief, from Property, than its present holders, the thrusters out, are likely to have in one case out of a hundred. Even admitting the Parchment Right of the poor, of two centuries and a half standing, to have been constitutionally quashed by the enactment of 1834, it has been declared by the highest legal authorities, that 'the right to live stands on a deeper foundation than any right to property can possibly do'.*
> – John Bowen, *The Russell Predictions on the Working Class*, 1850[1]

The introduction of the deeply controversial New Poor Law in 1834 radically changed the shape of social welfare in Britain. While the parish system had been uneven at best, the centralization of relief led to a depersonalization of aid, which diminished the sense of human responsibility among communities, while entrenching the concept of the deserving and undeserving poor. In their introduction to *Economic Women* (2014), Lana Dalley and Jill Rappoport argue that the New Poor Law is the best example of the 'turn away from *œconomy* and toward political economy, [in which] the gift practices associated with community care typically give way to less interpersonal notions of independent contract and self-help'.[2] Furthermore, the devastating ramifications of the infamous workhouses quickly became evident. John Bowen referred to the workhouses as murder and the New Poor Law as 'National contrivances for destroying the helpless'.³ He cites a writer in the *Edinburgh Review*, saying 'though we do not take these persons out of their houses and murder them, we do the same thing in effect', and criticizes the inhumane state of the workhouse: 'We *do* thrust legitimate claimants for relief, helpless infancy and destitute old age, into poisonous homes, and leave them there, with defective nourishment, to a lingering but certain death'.⁴ This defence of the most vulnerable members of the community stood against the harsher voices of political economy, government legislators and even some influential clergymen, who bought into the convenient 'belief that the right to relief threatened the nation's prosperity' and that 'recognition of such a right would upset the social hierarchy'.⁵ In a speech to the House of Lords on 21 July 1834, Lord Chancellor Henry Brougham claimed that it was 'in defiance of the ordinary laws of nature, [that] the human lawgiver should decree, that all poor men have a right to live comfortably',⁶ while in 1841 the Reverend Thomas Spencer wrote, 'This natural right to a maintenance is… wholly imaginary… industry should have its food, and idleness its hunger'.⁷

Yet as much as this shift occurred in political, social and even religious thought in the nineteenth century, there remained impetus within some elements of society to support the vulnerable and to encourage community-based responsibility and relief. As Dalley and Rappoport observe, 'the rupture between old and new was never as clearly cut in practice as it was in theory'.⁸ Instead there remained a tension between moral and political economy that went beyond legislation. This was particularly true of the 'alternative economic practices' of women, which were 'often ridiculed as ladies' work, [but] frequently emerged out of suffering'.⁹ Elizabeth Gaskell wrote powerfully of the economic and social actions performed by women, often motivated by religious conviction, that epitomize 'efforts to both articulate and enact forms of mutually beneficial, ethical exchange'.[10] Although famously writing in the preface to *Mary Barton* (1848) to 'know nothing of political economy' before setting forth her powerful literary illustration of the science's flaws,[11] Gaskell's work is notable for the way in which she engages with the ethics of consumption and giving in the context of the practical theology of the established church – that is, the Church of England. Her fictional narratives express the complexities not only of political economy in practice, but of ethical choices in relation to social imbalances and the question of whom should be considered accountable and responsible for rectifying such imbalances – or even if to do so is ethically necessary.

Dietary abstinence and social empathy

Although Unitarian, Elizabeth Gaskell was ecumenical in her social, theological and literary influences. She wrote with a voice that acknowledged both dissenting and establishment narratives, thus engaging with the complexities of social understanding and socio-economic privilege. As Elizabeth Ludlow has observed, because scholarship has focused primarily on Gaskell's Unitarianism, her nuanced relationship with religion and theology, especially the presence of Methodism in her fiction, has been largely ignored.[12] Ludlow suggests that this neglect is primarily due to 'the apparent incompatibility between [Methodism's] emphasis on enthusiasm with Unitarian principles of rational thought'.[13] Yet Gaskell's dissatisfaction with 'dogmatic hard Unitarianism',[14] alongside the little noted movement in which 'some Methodist congregations came over to Unitarianism'[15] suggests a 'cross-fertilisation' of Unitarianism and Methodism that illuminates Gaskell's complex theology.[16] Another seemingly theological anomaly is Gaskell's engagement with millennialism. Yet while Gaskell's millennialism is more understood as the necessity to 'imitate Christ and actively bring about the renewal of the world' than Christina Rossetti's Trinitarian millennialism of Christ the divine, it remains that they both believed in a practical theology that made the members of the Church accountable for both the spiritual and physical well-being of society. Gaskell's ecumenism is similar to Josephine Butler's in that the outworking of renewal and social justice was much more crucial than doctrinal debates. Importantly, Ludlow points out that the presence of millennialism amongst Gaskell's working-class characters is not a representation of passivity, although some '[accept] their earthly sufferings', but 'a call to challenge hierarchy and the ordering of society'.[17]

In Gaskell's work, the complexity of her practical theology is often revealed through food consumption and food exchange. In *Cranford* (1853) for example, the main reason why starvation is avoided is because the community is infused with an understanding that the way to show sympathy and care for others is a general restraint of consumption. The characters display an ethical position that causes them to look outward, thinking of others, rather than protecting or performing their own imagined security. Particularly in cross-class sympathy, characters like Miss Matty are willing to struggle directly with the ethics of giving and receiving, as well as abstaining, all of which come from a standpoint of looking outward to the community. Such questions include the extent to which one should refuse gifts out of a sense of whether the giver can afford them, or the potential for the receiver to reciprocate, or if it is helpful to others for an individual to refrain from consumption. In 'Gentry, Gender, and the Moral Economy' (2013), Kathryn Gleadle argues that 'dietary abstinence' is primarily a psychological means to engage with economic crisis – that is, by deliberately abstaining from a substance, one can become more sympathetic to the plight of those who have no choice in their abstinence.[18] Ilana Blumberg takes this idea further, asking questions regarding what kinds of 'economic exchange might be productive of ethical human relations', as well as what kinds of wealth are permissible in order to 'escape the risks of unethical possession or circulation' – that is, what can one possess without being unethical? A certain level of wealth could be considered necessary to have the means to help others, but when does wealth become excessive?[19] In Gaskell's view, it seems that ethical wealth has less to do with the product itself or its quantity, and more to do with the character's attitude toward using it. As Regenia Gagnier states, 'ethics... means our responsibility toward others', and so the ethics of consumption are inherently tied to the way in which our consumption affects the consumption of others, especially those who are considered socially and economically vulnerable.[20]

Yet motivations are often complicated. A significant example is found in *Ruth* (1853) when, after Ruth's son, Leonard, is baptized, Mr Benson, the minister, invites Jemima Bradshaw to share tea with his family. Jemima runs home to ask her father for permission, which is granted with the following qualification: 'Take no sugar in your tea, Jemima. I am sure the Bensons ought not to be able to afford sugar, with their means. And do not eat much; you can have plenty at home on your return; remember Mrs Denbigh's keep must cost them a great deal'.[21] On the surface it could appear that Mr Bradshaw is concerned for the Bensons' welfare, and wants to remind his daughter to be similarly concerned and careful: to restrain her consumption out of consideration for her neighbours. It is, however, problematic because of the ways in which Mr Bradshaw uses shared eating and gift-giving to assert his economic privilege and social power throughout the narrative. On the simplest level, he is controlling his daughter's taste preferences. She may prefer sweetened tea, but he is denying her that option out of a perceived idea of what the Bensons should or should not be able to consume for themselves, and therefore what would be appropriate for them to offer their guests. That has implications for Jemima's ability to make choices in general, and acts as a symbol of how their relationship works in the novel. Yet even further, when Mr Bradshaw says that the Bensons should not be able to afford sugar, he is trying to control the Bensons' economic, and therefore social, position. Their social relationship depends, for Bradshaw, on his ability to assert and maintain a higher level of economic privilege, a position from which he can choose to be their benefactor. He thinks that the 'Bensons ought not to be able to afford sugar, with their means'. As their benefactor, as well as the owner of the financial company that looks after Mr Benson's shares, Bradshaw not only knows exactly what those means are, he perceives that he has a right to control how they are spent. His instruction, therefore, emerges not from a concern that the Bensons might not be able to afford sugar and his daughter might strain their economic means; rather he is seeking to control how the Bensons spend their income – what purchases they can make – thus diminishing their economic agency. Sugar is deemed to be a luxury and, as such, Mr Bradshaw thinks it is inappropriate for the Bensons to buy it.

Mr Bradshaw does not actually have the authority to control what the Bensons buy; he can, however, manipulate his daughter to prevent her from participating in something that he considers to be an excess. By virtue of his social privilege, his daughter may consume sugar, but only on his terms and in spaces that he allows, such as in their own home. He therefore uses his authority over his daughter to assert power over the domestic and economic spaces of others – a behaviour that aligns with his profession as an investment broker, in which he is responsible for controlling the finances of others. His attitude is passed on to an extreme in his son, who sees his right to steal from the investors in the company, which ultimately disrupts Bradshaw's power. In this way, Gaskell disciplines the misuse and abuse of food restraint. She draws together food ethics and ethical economics in a way that reflects the 'moral webs' of ethical foodscapes that Goodman, Maye and Holloway articulate.[22] For food restraint to be ethical, there must be genuine outward-focused concern. The ethical imperative of food consumption is determined by how that consumption affects others. Importantly it recognizes that an individual's consumption does, in fact, both directly and indirectly impact other individuals and therefore has the potential to affect society more generally. Yet through her fictional illustration, Gaskell represents the complexities in defining what is ethical: there are different ethics, or ideas of goodness, working in competition with each other. The economic fairness to farmers is in tension with the economic precarity of consumers; there is also the challenge of healthful fresh food versus cheap food; and there is also the idea of choice, and access to choice, which brings into tension ideas of necessity and luxury.

The choice of sugar in *Ruth* is significant, acting more broadly as a symbol for both ethical economics and ethical eating. Sugar held very specific social and political meaning in nineteenth-century Britain, tied to the nation's long history of imperialism and colonization, in which the commodity of sugar represents social luxury and privilege. It reached a crisis point in the late eighteenth century with the Anti-Saccharite Movement boycotting sugar in protest of the slave labour that enabled the West Indian sugar plantations to maintain an edge in the market. At this time, one's attitude toward sugar consumption grew to be equated with one's social conscience. In *Pathological Bodies* (2013), Corinna Wagner describes the late eighteenth-century understanding of the connection between the taste for sugar and social conscience through her reading of Shelley's notes to his famous poem *Queen Mab*, which were published separately as an essay in 1813 with the title *A Vindication of Natural Diet*. In this essay, Shelley argues,

> On a natural system of diet we should require no spices from India; no wines from Portugal, Spain, France, or Madeira; none of those multitudinous articles of luxury, for which every corner of the globe is rifled, and which are the causes of so much individual rivalship, such as calamitous and sanguinary national disputes.[23]

Wagner argues that in this perspective the 'consumption of foreign foodstuffs supports the injustices inherent in empire and makes otherwise autonomous, freedom-loving nations dependent and vulnerable', and further that 'Exotic tastes lead to inhumane acts and greedy politics, at home and abroad'. Moving onto Shelley's *Oedipus Tyrannus*, Wagner states, 'Shelley portrays a homegrown form of injustice that feeds on, and is fed by, global exploitation and violence'.[24]

Wagner goes on to discuss the role of the 'public campaign against the consumption of sugar and its relation to privilege and luxury' in relation to the anti-slavery movement that led to the abolition of the slave trade in 1807.[25] It was another thirty years, though, before slavery itself was abolished in the Empire. The setting of Gaskell's *Ruth* within the late 1830s and 1840s is crucial, then, because it positions the narrative within a key moment in the politics of sugar and slavery. When the Empire's plantation owners agreed to relinquish slavery in 1837, they did so with the understanding that their trade would be protected from tariffs, and therefore they would have cheaper import duties. The way in which sugar from the West Indian plantations was protected was similar to the way that the Corn Laws had protected British domestic grain produce. However, during the same sitting of Parliament that the British government repealed the Corn Laws, they also removed the import tax protection on British West Indian sugar. The Sugar Duties Act of 1846 meant that British-owned sugar could no longer compete with other international traders, especially those in South America that were still using slave labour. There was a cost to the British Empire's moral choice that impacted the reception of sugar. The plantation owners felt betrayed by the British government, while the people in Britain who purchased sugar were torn between ideas of national loyalty (by supporting British produce, even if it was grown thousands of miles away) or the cheaper 'foreign' options – foreign options that maintained the unpalatable, unethical connections to slavery. This latter perception further erased the fact that there was little sense of responsibility among ex-slaveowners to care for the well-being of their now ex-slave labour force. For consumers, being able to afford (seemingly) ethical sugar was a mark of social and economic privilege.

The way in which the British Government tied together the repeal of the Corn Laws and the passing of the Sugar Duties Act made a powerful statement regarding necessity and luxury: corn and wheat were staples of the British diet, while sugar was, arguably, non-essential; but the suggested correlation in the joint legislation meant that what was considered necessary to the diet was given equal importance to what was considered a non-essential luxury. While making choices about what food to buy, the purchaser is expected not just to consider what their own family needs in balance with what they can afford, they are also expected to consider how their purchase choices are going to affect, both economically and socially, the suppliers of the commodities, as well as those whose labour produces it. Therefore, the way that Mr Bradshaw focuses on sugar when he admonishes Jemima is pertinent to the understanding of ethical economics and ethical foodscapes throughout the text. When eating, and particularly when experiencing shared eating, questions of how much to eat, what to eat, and who to eat with speak directly to an individual's social agency and privilege, as well as their sense of social responsibility and justice.

Jemima Bradshaw's fraught sympathy operates in stark contrast to the manipulative nature of her father. Both his authority and Jemima's social education limit the means by which she can exercise sympathy, both because of her position in his household and the structures of morality that he imposes. Jemima's response, however, reflects her willingness to grapple with her own privilege in relation to the comparative poverty of others, and this then permeates her perspective not just on economic privilege in the text, but also the social privilege she enjoys as opposed to the social vulnerability that Ruth experiences, and the ways in which moral structures can operate in tension with or even in opposition to what might be considered ethical. Jemima's later relationship with the exposed Ruth is therefore foreshadowed in her awkward sharing of tea with the Bensons. To what extent should Jemima *not* consume in order to save the Bensons the expense of feeding her, or does such restraint deny the Bensons the social agency that is outworked through the gift of hospitality? Is there an element of social pride or perceived morality in abiding by her father's command? Following Bradshaw's order to take no sugar in her tea,

> Jemima returned considerably sobered, and very much afraid of her hunger leading her to forget Mr Benson's poverty. Meanwhile Miss Benson and Sally, acquainted with Mr Benson's invitation to Jemima, set about making some capital tea-cakes on which they piqued themselves. They both enjoyed the offices of hospitality; and were glad to place some home-made tempting dainty before their guests... It was a disappointment to Miss Benson's kind hospitable expectation when Jemima, as hungry as a hound, confined herself to one piece of the cake which her hostess had had such pleasure in making... This evening her spirits were dampened by Jemima's refusal to eat! Poor Jemima! the cakes were so good, and she was so hungry, but still she refused.[26]

Gaskell's adjectival use of 'capital' to describe the tea-cakes is pointed. The tea-cakes represent both economic and social capital, and Bradshaw's instructions to Jemima encourage her to reject the capital of the Bensons, and therefore their economic and social agency. That, however, is not Jemima's intention, but rather to be respectful, even though the refusal leads to disappointment for everyone involved in the meal – apart from Bradshaw. Bradshaw is determined to deny the Bensons' capital, even if that means waste. The narrative ironically focalizes 'Poor Jemima', though, which reasserts that although everyone is disappointed, she would still be able to go home and eat her fill.

'Elegant economy' and mutual restraint

In contrast to Jemima's angst and Miss Benson's disappointment in *Ruth*, in *Cranford*, the 'elegant economy' practised by the town's inhabitants is made possible because they are on an equal social, if not economic, footing. In the almost idyllic setting, the main characters never speak of their own poverty and instead focus on the generosity they are able to show to others; and while their generosity is limited, their tacit understanding of each other's limited capacity means that the reciprocal generosity extends the possibilities of community and common feeling, rather than causing division. From the beginning, the narrator establishes that

> [A] few of the gentlefolks of Cranford were poor, and had some difficulty in making both ends meet; but they were like the Spartans, and concealed their smart under a smiling face. We none of us spoke of money, because that subject savoured of commerce and trade, and though some might be poor, we were all aristocratic. The Cranfordians had that kindly *esprit de corps* which made them overlook all deficiencies in success when some among them tried to conceal their poverty.[27]

The discretion of the Cranfordians is enacted upon the reader: the narrative does not disclose which of the gentlefolk are the few who are poor. Respectability in Cranford is found in 'this general but unacknowledged poverty, and this very much acknowledged gentility'.[28] The point of difference lies in their common feeling, manifested in their desire to protect one another's dignity.

Common feeling in Cranford is made possible because poverty is considered common to all. Even for those who are perhaps not impoverished, they conduct themselves in an understated way so as not to embarrass or put the pressure of reciprocity on their neighbours. In this way, *Cranford* resists realism – it imagines a society in which there are little if any class differentiations, or there is a perceived equality across classes. One example is when Miss Matty's servant, Martha, takes over Miss Matty's house, and Miss Matty becomes Martha's lodger. This movement follows Martha insisting on buying the ingredients herself to make a pudding for Miss Matty when she realizes that Miss Matty cannot afford it. The class transition here is treated very smoothly by the narrative, deflecting the class implications. The deflection is made possible out of Martha's compassion – as a poorer member of the community, she has sympathy for Miss Matty's new impoverished position. This links back to Gaskell's preface to *Mary Barton* where she says that only the poor care for the poor, although Miss Matty's neighbours also secretly get together to try to provide more for her. They do this out of a recognition of her social status, rather than her fluctuating economic means. It is important to note that what makes Cranford a fascinating study is the way in which the inhabitants redefine appropriate behaviour and hospitality with the tacit understanding of mutual limited economic means. As a social body, what affects one member affects them all. Excess and waste become explicitly offensive in a way that deflects limited provision at, for example, a dinner party, away from not being able to afford to provide more, instead considering large portions or a wide range of choices as obscene. Being frugal – or economical – is more highly valued than displays of wealth. Elegance is valued above lavishness. This motive, however, can come in tension with being hospitable.

Much of Gaskell's fiction shows a concern for the tensions between being hospitable and being frugal, fears and disgust at excess, and the ironic offense of hospitality, which is made possible through the misunderstandings and miscommunications of social expectations. Two key moments that display these complexities are first, in *Cranford*, where the narrator, Mary, describes Miss Barker the milliner's excess (in Cranfordian terms) in hosting a tea, and the ironic way in which Mary talks about the politeness displayed by the other characters in accepting Miss Barker's misplaced hospitality, in spite of them being offended at being offered so much, and the second in *North and South* (1854–5), when Margaret goes to the Thorntons' dinner party. This dinner party occurs when the workers are striking – and many of them starving – and the guest list includes the other millowners in the district. Margaret is offended by the excess of provision at the dinner when there are so many people suffering. In *Cranford*, the offense lies in that the *guests* might be poor – and therefore potentially not able to reciprocate. In *North and South*, it is offensive because *others* who do not have the same level of social privilege are poor, and it therefore seems insensitive to feast and to waste food when others in such close physical proximity, although not of the same social class, do not have access to bare dietary necessities.

In *Cranford*, it is evident that Miss Barker does not understand the social mores of her neighbours. She seeks to win them over with the luxuries and excesses of hospitality. Mary, the narrator, observes, 'The tea-tray was abundantly loaded. I was pleased to see it, I was so hungry; but I was afraid the ladies present might think it vulgarly heaped up'.[29] One of the ironies of this passage, like with Jemima Bradshaw in *Ruth*, is that it focalizes a character as being hungry, but not in actual danger of starvation. Both Mary and Jemima are put in a position of being forced by perceived etiquette to refrain from eating as much as they want, even though there is plenty of food – even an excess of food – placed before them. With ironic fortune in *Cranford*, however, 'Mrs Jamieson was kindly indulgent to Miss Barker's want of knowledge of the customs of high life; and, to spare her feelings, ate three large pieces of seed-cake'.[30] Mary's account of Mrs Jamieson shows a kind fondness toward what is implied as her greed. Yet the way it is presented also reveals that there is a real anxiety regarding whether one should eat or not eat out of politeness to the host, to prevent waste, or to maintain the general consideration for the other members of the community also ensconced in this moment, as well as struggling with concerns over polite consumption and the potential or lack thereof for reciprocity. Mary continues her account of the supper:

> Another tray! 'Oh, gentility!' thought I, 'can you endure this last shock?' For Miss Barker had ordered... all sorts of good things for supper – scalloped oysters, potted lobsters, jelly, a dish called 'little Cupids', (which was in great favour with the Cranford ladies; although too expensive to be given, except on solemn and state occasions...). In short, we were evidently to be feasted with all that was sweetest and best; and we thought it better to submit graciously, even at the cost of our gentility – which never ate suppers in general – but which, like most non-supper eaters, was particularly hungry on all special occasions.[31]

Mary's ironic narrative voice is particularly useful in expressing the tension between being able to experience sensory taste and the restraint exerted by aesthetic taste, or social protocol, which is described in terms of taste, appropriateness and 'elegant economy', concepts that become interchangeable. The ironic tone reveals the way in which excess becomes justified through a rhetoric of politeness and respectfulness. Although the food is 'vulgarly heaped up', Mrs Jamieson and the other women are 'kindly indulgent' in that they eat the food, even though they secretly maintain a moral judgement on Miss Barker for being so excessive. This is a way of having their cake and eating it, too – they can justify to themselves the lack of reciprocity they will show through their belief that it was Miss Barker who behaved inappropriately, whereas they were generous in the way that they did not say anything to her and were polite enough to eat the provision – even to the clear excess of three pieces of seed-cake.

The language is comedic, but underlying the rhetoric is the suggestion that as much as the women of Cranford perform what they believe to be an ethical economy toward food and hospitality, they continue to desire more. They are not hypocrites; rather they act in tacit diplomacy. They understand that the social performance, and the suspension of disbelief, is their means of sustaining community and common feeling. As much as their performance described in occasions of shared eating is humorous, the same motive comes across in seemingly more serious situations, such as when they come together to secretly provide more for Miss Matty's income when she loses her shares in the bank. It is a similar performance: formalities in holding a meeting; a type of secret ballot where they write how much they can offer; and then the women who come privately to Mary to apologize for not offering more, and their reasoning behind it. Although these actions, too, can be read as comedy, they also show the important tact of this society that consists in privately acknowledging the restraints and limitations of others, while the women do not verbalize it out of respect. In this way, they maintain each other's dignity and, importantly, social agency through rewriting elegance and appropriate behaviour when it is not possible for agency to be exerted through economic means.

North and South also constructs social agency through diplomacy, but diplomacy in this novel looks quite different from that in *Cranford*. Such difference could be read in a gendered way: the diplomacy of men versus the diplomacy of women; but there are also the differences between diplomacy within a particular class – that is, the women of Cranford being socially equal – versus the cross-class diplomacy that eventually occurs between Robert Thornton and Nicholas Higgins, as well as the constructs of social and economic understanding and practices in the north as opposed to the south. When Margaret, the southerner, attends the dinner party at the Thorntons with the millowners of the area, she is offended by what she considers the excess of food provided, particularly given that this dinner party takes place while the workers are striking and Milton on the whole is in economic crisis. Mr Thornton himself is actually very conscious of how inappropriate having the dinner party is – more from a stance of his own financial position than thinking of social politics – but sees value in having a splendid dinner if it must be had. Gaskell carefully juxtaposes the conflicting mores of hospitality:

> Margaret, with her London cultivation of taste, felt the number of delicacies to be oppressive; one half of the quantity would have been enough, and the effect lighter and more elegant. But it was one of Mrs Thornton's rigorous laws of hospitality, that of each separate dainty enough should be provided for all the guests to partake, if they felt inclined. Careless to abstemiousness in her daily habits, it was part of her pride to set a feast before such of her guests as cared for it. Her son shared this feeling. He had never known – though he might have imagined, and had the capability to relish – any kind of society but that which depended on an exchange of superb meals: and even now, though he was denying himself the personal expenditure of an unnecessary sixpence, and had more than once regretted that the invitations for this dinner had been sent out, as it was to be, he was glad to see the old magnificence of preparation.[32]

Margaret's 'London cultivation of taste' resonates with the elegant economy of the women in *Cranford* – she believes that it would be more appropriate in general to have less available – the 'effect [would be] lighter and more elegant'. The passage is uncomfortably silent on the impoverishment of the workers, instead focusing on the financial precarity of the Thorntons, a move perhaps seeming distasteful in itself, but which reinforces that even the wealth Thornton was able to make for himself is tenuous.

Within the 'rigorous law of hospitality' shown by Mrs Thornton and her son, there is a form of diplomacy: in providing an impressive dinner for their guests, they create a bond of community in which there is a sense of obligation: not necessarily to provide a feast of the same standard (although that would probably come into play), but an obligation to engage in discussion around how to solve their mutual problem with the strikers. It is more difficult for one to be rude and abusive to one's host when one has been treated with luxury.

Furthermore, through a display of wealth, Thornton puts himself in a position of power and authority over his peers. This is not unlike Mr Bradshaw's use of wealth in *Ruth*; however, the difference between the two men is that where Thornton uses his wealth to persuade his social equals, Bradshaw uses it to manipulate those who are in a more vulnerable economic and social position. The valuable purpose behind the Thorntons' dinner party is highlighted later in the novel when Margaret is back in London. While the first dinner party seems oppressive to her, she later learns the importance of the discussions held there, in comparison to the inane discussions that take place in London, for all the more delicate or elegant setting and provision:

> These dinners were delightful; but even here Margaret's dissatisfaction found her out... They talked about art in a merely sensuous way, dwelling on outside effects, instead of allowing themselves to learn what it has to teach. They lashed themselves up into an enthusiasm about high subjects in company, and never thought about them when they were alone; they squandered their capabilities of appreciation into a mere flow of appropriate words.[33]

Margaret learns that shared eating is not merely about the quantity or quality of the foods available, but the purpose behind the eating. While she abhorred the waste in Milton, in London she observes a different kind of waste: a waste of human intellectual and moral energy, even if the provided fare is more moderate. The ethics of shared eating are revealed to be less about what is offered in terms of food, but the moral agency and will that are produced through purposeful consumption.

Purposeful shared eating and hospitality

In *Making Sense of Taste* (1999), Carolyn Korsmeyer argues that while 'eating is often praised for its role in hospitality and formation of community, the sustenance of social bonds through shared eating occurs against a backdrop of disturbing moral significance'.[34] She also suggests that 'the intimacy of eating… knits together those who eat' because there is a presumption of social equality between those who eat together.[35] In Shakespeare's *The Merchant of Venice*, Shylock tells Bassanio, 'I will buy with you, sell with you, talk with you, and so following; but I will not eat with you, drink with you, nor pray with you'.[36] Trade inherently suggests power relations, but eating together suggests equality and community. Even more, the material, physical act of eating is connected to a spiritual relationship. The way that Mr Bradshaw conducts himself in relation to food in *Ruth* is as an extension of trade: he uses the socializing aspects of food to manipulate, which goes as far as him asserting his economic and social position over the spiritual authority of his religious minister, Mr Benson. This is revealed in his withholding of his presence from the family pew, as well as with whom he allows his family to eat. It is only after Ruth has passed Bradshaw's 'test' of seeming to show 'economy by itself, without any soul or spirit in it to make it living and holy' that she finds 'merit in his eyes', and is invited to join Mr and Miss Benson in coming to tea.[37] It is also important to note that while the Bensons are regularly invited to tea at the Bradshaws, early in the narrative it is made clear to the reader that Mr Bradshaw rarely deigns to join them. Although he does not forbid his daughter from sharing food with the Bensons, he attempts, successfully, to restrict the extent to which she is able to participate in this seemed equality. The poignant angst of the miscommunication that Jemima experiences with Miss Benson, between Jemima's desire to restrain her appetite due to perceived ethics and sympathy, and Miss Benson's desire to show hospitality and kinship, is made possible through the fact that while shared eating implies equality, their relationship is far from equal: Mr Bradshaw has forbidden any occurrence of common feeling.

Gaskell's most successful example of shared eating, diplomacy and cross-class sympathy is found in *North and South*. In this novel, she provides the most optimistic vision, with a different kind of exchange – one that is more open and allows for equal human footing across class boundaries, rather than the secrecy and performance of *Cranford*, or the power struggle and manipulation of Bradshaw in *Ruth*. As much as the women of Cranford seek to protect each other's dignity through their secrecy and social performance, they cannot escape the fact that secrecy suggests shame. In *North and South*, however, the open acknowledgement of social position and economic struggle leads to a different kind of respect, illustrated through the relationship that develops between Thornton and Nicholas Higgins. This relationship culminates in Thornton, not just agreeing to Nicholas's suggestion of the workers' mess hall, but also eating with the workers there. Importantly, it is Thornton's determination not to infringe on the individual agency of his workers that enables shared eating, mutual respect and common feeling. He tells Mr Bell:

> 'I was very scrupulous, at first, in confining myself to the mere purchasing part, and even in that I rather obeyed the men's orders, conveyed through the housekeeper, than went with my own judgment. At one time, the beef was too large, at another the mutton was not fat enough. I think they saw how careful I was to leave them free, and not to intrude my own ideas on them; so, one day, two or three of the men – my friend Higgins among them – asked me if I would not come in and take a snack. It was a very busy day, but I saw that the men would be hurt if, after making the advance, I didn't meet them half-way, so I went in, and never made a better dinner in my life... If they had not asked me, I would no more have intruded on them than I'd have gone to the mess at the barracks without invitation'.[38]

Here, Thornton refers to Nicholas Higgins, not as his employee, not as his hand or worker, but as his friend. His willingness to respect the taste choices of his employees – to follow their judgement in the preparation and quality of the food provided – allows them to understand that he respects their human agency, and enables their dignity, even though they are not of an equal economic standing. Most importantly, it is Thornton's willingness to eat with his employees on equal terms that enables the strength of this relationship to continue: just as he ate with the other millowners and found a means to diplomacy over the earlier dinner party, he is able to discuss and resolve issues within his factory over a shared meal. Mr Bell ironically states, 'Nothing like the act of eating for equalizing men. Dying is nothing to it', and then tries to offer Thornton 10 pounds toward the kitchen.[39] Thornton refuses this gift on the grounds that he does not want to turn the dining hall into a charity. Mr Bell – a confirmed southerner, an old man of inherited means and therefore a more feudal mindset rather than understanding the new industrial world – misses the point: he does not understand that in his attempt at charity, he is removing the equality that Thornton and Higgins have worked to establish despite economic disparity.

Gaskell's variations in economic approaches suggest the complexities in real-life concerns surrounding human agency and privilege, as well as her acknowledgement that disparities in social power are inevitable. The challenges faced by individuals and institutions, not to mention communities and nations, persist. It is evident that one's ability to make choices depends on one's economic stability and security. Amartya Sen writes, 'A person's ability to avoid starvation will depend both on his ownership and on the exchange entitlement mapping that he faces', and adds:

> A general decline in food supply may indeed cause him to be exposed to hunger through a rise in food prices with an unfavourable impact on his exchange entitlement. Even when his starvation is *caused* by food shortage in this way, his immediate reason for starvation will be the decline in his exchange entitlement.[40]

'Exchange entitlement' means the individual's capacity to trade, so whether they have the income and means to buy the food they need, and the food they want. In most of Gaskell's fiction, there are few actually starving people at the centre of the narrative – actual starvation remains in the margins.[41] In *Ruth* there are the nameless homeless people Ruth observes when she is returning to Mrs Mason's after being at the ball; in *Cranford* there is even less direct starvation, although there is the hint of its possibility in the man who finds his bank notes are worthless, and Miss Matty gives him a sovereign in exchange; and in *North and South* there is Boucher and his family, as well as the many nameless workers who strike, not to mention the desperate Irish workers brought in by Thornton. They remain largely nameless, though, rather than being central characters. The way that poverty haunts the text from the margins acts to reinforce the constant *risk* of starvation and poverty that the main characters experience, which creates an anxiety that is at times more debilitating than the reality of poverty itself. Although they do not starve, their economic state is always precarious. The recognition of one's precarity, as a reflection of the vulnerability in others, is at the core of Victorian ethical food restraint, whether it is manifested as a social consciousness regarding what one should consume, a kind of elegant economy that is concerned for another's capacity to reciprocate, or a willingness to eat food that one would not normally consume in order to acknowledge a kinship and common feeling. The way in which Gaskell's fiction values common feeling in this way, manifested through food restraint, resonates strongly with Christina Rossetti's theology of fellow-feeling and the unity of the Body of Christ. Although coming from vastly different theological persuasions, Gaskell and Rossetti similarly find value in food restraint – whether referred to as 'elegant economy' or fasting – as a means of promoting a cohesive, functional and compassionate social body.

Notes

1. John Bowen, *The Russell Predictions on the Working Class, the National Debt, and the New Poor Law. Dissected* (London: Hatchard & Son, 1850), iv.
2. Lana L. Dalley and Jill Rappoport, 'Introducing Economic Women', in *Economic Women: Essays on Desire and Dispossession in Nineteenth-Century British Culture*, 1–21 (Columbus: Ohio State University Press, 2013), 4–5.
3. Bowen, *The Russell Predictions*, iii.
4. Ibid., iv.
5. Thomas A. Horne, '"The Poor Have a Claim Founded in the Law of Nature": William Paley and the Rights of the Poor', *Journal of the History of Philosophy*, 23.1 (1985): 52.
6. Qtd. In Ibid., 52.
7. Thomas Spencer, *Objections to the New Poor Law Answered, Part 4* (London: John Green, 1841), 4.
8. Dalley and Rappoport, 'Introducing Economic Women', 5.
9. Ibid.
10. Ibid.
11. Elizabeth Gaskell, Preface to *Mary Barton* (1848; Oxford: Oxford University Press, 1998), xxxvi.
12. Elizabeth Ludlow, 'Working-Class Methodism and Eschatological Anxiety in Elizabeth Gaskell's Fiction', *The Gaskell Journal*, 34 (2020): 25–40, 28.
13. Ibid., 29.
14. J.A.V. Chapple and Arthur Pollard, eds., *The Letters of Mrs Gaskell* (Manchester: Mandolin, 1997), 136.
15. Angus Easson, *Elizabeth Gaskell* (London: Routledge and Kegan Paul, 1979), 8–10.
16. Ludlow, 'Working-Class Methodism', 30.
17. Ibid., 27.
18. Kathryn Gleadle, 'Gentry, Gender, and the Moral Economy during the Revolutionary and Napoleonic Wars in Provincial England', in

Economic Women: Essays on Desire and Dispossession in Nineteenth-Century British Culture, ed. Lana L. Dalley and Jill Rappoport, 25–40 (Columbus: Ohio State University Press, 2013), 36.

19 Ilana Blumberg, 'Sacrificial Value: Beyond the Cash Nexus in George Eliot's *Romola*', in *Economic Women: Essays on Desire and Dispossession in Nineteenth-Century British Culture*, ed. Lana L. Dalley and Jill Rappoport, 60–74 (Columbus: Ohio State University Press, 2013), 61.

20 Regenia Gagnier, 'Economic Women in Their Time, Our Time, and the Future', Afterword in *Economic Women: Essays on Desire and Dispossession in Nineteenth-Century British Culture*, ed. Lana L. Dalley and Jill Rappoport, 219–24 (Columbus: Ohio State University Press, 2013), 224.

21 Elizabeth Gaskell *Ruth* (1853; London: Penguin, 1997), 151.

22 Michael K. Goodman, Damian Maye and Lewis Holloway, 'Ethical Foodscapes?: Premises, Promises, and Possibilities', *Environment and Planning*, 42 (2010): 1782–96, 1784.

23 Qtd in Corinna Wagner, *Pathological Bodies: Medicine and Political Culture* (Berkeley: University of California Press, 2013), 221.

24 Ibid., 221–2.

25 Ibid., 222.

26 Gaskell, *Ruth*, 151–2.

27 Elizabeth Gaskell, *Cranford* (1853; Oxford: Oxford University Press, 2011), 4–5.

28 Ibid., 5.

29 Ibid., 66.

30 Ibid.

31 Ibid., 67–8

32 Gaskell, *North and South* (1854–5; London: Penguin, 1995), 159.

33 Ibid., 397.

34 Carolyn Korsmeyer, *Making Sense of Taste: Food and Philosophy* (Ithaca: Cornell University Press, 1999), 9.

35 Ibid., 187.

36 William Shakespeare, *The Merchant of Venice* (1596–7; London: Penguin, 1965), Act I Sc. iii, ll. 33–5.

37 Gaskell, *Ruth*, 133.
38 Gaskell, *North and South*, 353–4.
39 Ibid., 354.
40 Amartya Sen, *Poverty and Famines: An Essay on Entitlement and Deprivation* (Oxford: Oxford University Press, 1981), 4.
41 *Mary Barton* is a notable exception to this claim.

2

Christina Rossetti, spiritual growth and social justice

The spiritualist makes individualism the centre of his system. Properly beginning with faith, he very improperly refines this quality to mere sentiment, being naturally jealous that it should be so material as to have any relation to definite work.
  – Robert Wilson Evans, *The Ministry of the Body*, 1847[1]

As a significant contributor to *Rivington's Theological Library*, a collection that was designed to 'restore to England the tradition of the primitive church', Robert Wilson Evans was a part of the same spirit of revival within the Anglican Church that inspired the Tractarian or Oxford Movement.[2] He was, however, critical of some of the more ascetic elements of the revival that seemed too closely aligned to Roman Catholicism, in particular what he saw as the effect of fasting on an individual's social vision. In general, he saw the 'undue abstraction, that is by spiritualism'[3] of more puritanical protestants and the 'extreme material grossness' of Roman Catholicism[4] both leading to a narrowing of faith. Paradoxically, it seems that the combination of the material asceticism of Romanism combined with what Evans refers to as spiritualism is the most dangerous state: where the material act reinforces an inward perspective that focuses on one's own spiritual state to the detriment of connections with nature and the community. As 'Outward ordinances are evaporated into mere inward experiences, and particularity of the body is lost in the vague and general contemplation of the spirit',[5] Evans sees an increase of the 'unhealthy state of the public mind', which he describes as a 'disease' that needs to be remedied.[6] He goes on to suggest that the act of fasting is, contrary to the true doctrine of Christianity, egotistically performative: 'there comes a resort to greater affectation still of spirituality, as being the more efficacious from its greater abstraction, until every thing outward and practical is lost in selfish vagueness and unsocial unprofitableness'.[7]

In principle, Christina Rossetti's materialist theology aligns with Evans's, primarily in regard to the importance of spiritual practices leading to social justice practices. However, regarding fasting, Rossetti's view was more attune with Edward Pusey and the Oxford Movement. Fasting was a means not just to a healthy body and soul, but an act by which one is refined spiritually in such a way as to recognize one's connection to the Body of Christ and, crucially, one's divine responsibility to care for that Body as well as one's own. Furthermore, the regulation of fasting through liturgy helps to moderate such extremes to keep the faster's vision outward on the purpose of social justice, rather than being falsely led inward.

Rossetti's materialist theology and fasting

Following Lynda Palazzo's groundbreaking work in *Christina Rossetti's Feminist Theology* (2002) and Mary Arseneau's *Recovering Christina Rossetti: Female Community and Incarnational Poetics* (2004), there has been a concentrated effort to recover Rossetti not just as a poet, but as a theologian. Moving beyond seeing her work as repressive, scholars such as Emma Mason and Kirstie Blair have brought to the fore the role of the Tractarian Doctrine of Reserve as the mode of Rossetti's poetry and, indeed, poetry and poetic restraint as central to Rossetti's theology,[8] while Elizabeth Ludlow has defined her as 'a creative theologian concerned with bringing her perception of God's love and justice to an "arrogant England" that she perceived as increasingly enmeshed in consumerism and imperialism'.[9] What has been rarely addressed is the influence of Eastern Orthodox theology on Rossetti's work, and in particular its relationship to her perspective on fasting. Ludlow observes the importance of Orthodox saints in the Tractarian contemplative writings, as well as their specific influence on key Tractarians John Mason Neale and Richard Frederick Littledale, who were both influential in Rossetti's theology.[10] Similarly Emma Mason notes the role of the Eastern Fathers in Edward Pusey's works, who was also Rossetti's friend and theological colleague, stating that it was through Pusey that 'Rossetti grasped the profound importance of the Church Fathers'.[11] Orthodox theology was central to the development of materialist theology in the Anglican church, emerging from the Oxford Movement, not only in its emphasis on moderation, reserve and poetry, but the belief in the Real Presence and bodily resurrection, which underpinned the sense of unity in the Body of Christ as well as the importance of a social justice that recognized the need to provide welfare for the physical body as much as for the soul. Most crucially, Eastern Orthodoxy's incarnational theology influenced the Oxford Movement's understanding of a sacred earth in which all of creation was the Body of Christ Incarnate. It was therefore through the 'participatory faith [of] the Cappadocian Fathers' that Rossetti developed her own incarnational understanding of 'participation with creation, the saints, and God', and of poetry as a theological mechanism that communicated a 'unified creation... the cosmos as the living and dynamic body of God'.[12] This 'cosmic entanglement of things in God' was the foundation of both Rossetti's theology and her social vision.[13]

In the Oxford Movement's desire to return to the primitive Church and the Church Fathers, although so frequently (and fearfully) associated with Roman Catholicism, their theology was much more aligned to Eastern Orthodoxy. It is impossible not to read the Oxford Movement through the context of the Emancipation of Roman Catholicism in 1829; yet the emphasis on Roman Catholicism has meant that the connection to Eastern Orthodoxy has been largely ignored. As Geoffrey Rowell notes, the 'changing character of the state', in both parliament and the church, in the 1820s and 1830s led to a reassessment of Anglicanism, which underpinned the Oxford Movement:

> How did the Church of England stand in relation to 'popular Protestantism' on the one hand and the Church of Rome on the other? What was the relationship between the Church of England and the church of the first four centuries with which Anglican formularies claimed a special kinship? If the foundations of Anglican theology lay not just in Scripture and a simple 'Bible-Christianity' but in the Catholic creeds and the theological and liturgical tradition of the Early Church, how ought Anglican theology and practice to reflect and continue that heritage?[14]

Indeed, as much as it has been argued that the Oxford Movement sought to return to an English Catholicism that predated the Reformation, it is perhaps more accurate to say that they were seeking to establish an English Orthodox Church. The connection between the two traditions and liturgies was continually reinforced throughout the nineteenth century, with the establishment of the Anglican and Eastern Orthodox Churches Union in 1864 by, among others, John Mason Neale, who, while he studied at Cambridge, was heavily influenced by the Oxford Movement, and then later the movement toward reunification of the three branches – Anglicanism, Eastern Orthodoxy and Roman Catholicism – which Edward Pusey championed. Like Pusey, Rossetti's theology rests most comfortably within Orthodox traditions in her desire for the authenticity of the primitive Church. In *Smyrna's Ashes* (2012), Michelle Tusan refers to 'an imagined kinship with Eastern Christians', and argues that the 'opposition of Eastern Orthodoxy to Rome secured these connections by forging a sense of solidarity against a Catholic other'.[15] Although Rossetti does not explicitly engage with this issue, what becomes clear is a distinct resonance – or solidarity – between her theology and Orthodoxy, with her appreciation of 'solemn but simple' liturgical rites and 'rich liturgical poetry',[16] while her lived practice displays an inclusive Catholicism toward the Three Branches.

The key element of Orthodoxy that influences materialist theology is its respect for the body – the body's sacredness, and thus the sacredness of all bodies – which then feeds into other areas such as attitudes toward consumption, social justice and public health. Materialist theology defines spiritual matters in material terms – their material impact on the Body of Christ. It therefore displays a willingness to grapple with the material. What do spiritual terms mean in a material sense? What should be seen as a result of the spirit? Todd Williams brings Rossetti's materialist theology to the fore when he writes that 'Rossetti can only receive spiritual knowledge indirectly as a physical being relating to a natural environment. Her knowledge of and belief in God, then, are achieved through affective responses to objects in the world and an embodied relation to them'. He goes on to add, 'Rossetti conceives of her spiritual self through her embodied self'.[17] This concept of affective embodiment relates to Rossetti's view of fasting as a spiritual practice in two ways: first, in the belief that spiritual growth occurs through affective embodiment, and further that spiritual growth cannot occur without an affective, active response to the world around oneself. Second, given the intimate connectedness between body and soul, the sensation of fasting in and of itself can create compassion for the hungry. The medical doctor George Moore suggests this when he writes of 'choos[ing] not merely according to appetite, but to conviction',[18] and more explicitly about the effects of fasting causing a sympathetic focus on the stomachs of others through one's own abstinence:

> It is not the senses merely that may be rendered more acute by effort of mind. Attention to any part of the body is capable of *exalting the sensibility* of that part, or of causing the consciousness concerning its state to be affected in a new manner. Thus a man may attend to his stomach till he feels the process of digestion.[19]

Later Moore connects such a bodily process more explicitly with the theological: 'Sympathy is the natural check which the Almighty puts upon charitable self. In spite of themselves, there are few who have not felt compassion for others. This affords a beautiful proof both of the beneficence of our Maker, and the power of mind over the body'.[20]

Anna Krugovoy Silver notes that the High Anglican approach to food consumption and food restraint was that 'People must eat because the body requires food, but they should eat only as much as their health demands, not merely for pleasure'.[21] Yet this pragmatism toward consumption should not be mistaken for neglecting the sensory aesthetic of eating. Indeed, for High Anglicanism, as for Orthodoxy, aesthetic appreciation is equated with a consciousness of the beauty of creation, and therefore a significant means of worshipping God. In her appreciation of 'the whole vegetable creation', Rossetti imagines what would be lost if food was merely fuel for the body, not appreciated for its beauty:

> Fancy what it would become if it went on supplying all that is necessary, but not our necessaries in their actual familiar garb of beauty! Suppose we no longer had cornfields and orchards, but a magazine of 'constituents,' gluten, starch, saccharine matter, what not… While as the case stands our study of 'all green things' may fitly become a study of beauty and pleasure, an exercise of thankfulness.[22]

While in this passage Rossetti is referring to food in nature – before it becomes food – this is still important in her theology of consumption; for the ability to appreciate the connection of the food on the plate to nature, and the substance of God in Creation, is central to eating or not eating as a form of sacred worship. In *Letter and Spirit* (1883), it cannot be considered incidental that the celebrated poet uses the language of gluttony to suggest what can be learned on a metaphysical level through the visceral sensory experience of eating or not eating. When she writes of the weak-willed prophet Balaam's 'indulged distaste for the Divine Will',[23] she conflates the gluttony and general indulgence of her society with a distaste for God; and this emphasis on taste, rather than on the stomach, leads to the sin of Disinclination: 'Disinclination makes them (so to say) graze the hedge on one side or other at every step; thorns catch them, stones half trip them up, a perpetual dust attends their footsteps, grace and comeliness of aspect vanish'.[24] With the biblical precedent of something being sweet to the tongue but bitter to the stomach,[25] Rossetti alludes to an attentiveness to the stomach both in terms of resisting physical excess that the body does not require in response to the growing consumerism of middle-class society, but also out of a consciousness and compassion for those who go without.

The ethics of fasting from the perspective of materialist theology and spiritual growth come from this double consciousness of one's own needs and the need of others, taken with consideration of what one can command. 'Zeal', writes Rossetti, 'knows little, and goes on to know less and less, of self-indulgence and personal luxuries'.[26] Importantly for Rossetti, fasting is not about embracing material abjection, but about 'overcom[ing]' oneself, giving biblical examples of figures who prayed and fasted, and, 'that done, their circumstances turned out favourable'.[27] In overcoming oneself, the focus should not be on the favourable outcome *for* oneself, leaving that outcome to the Divine Will: 'the paramount motive for what we do or leave undone – if, that is, we aim at either acting or forebearing worthily – is love: not fear, or self-interest, or even hatred of sin, or sense of duty, but direct filial love to God'.[28] In Rossetti's theology, the way to demonstrate such love toward God is to show love to God's creatures: her fellow-feeling toward the Body of Christ. While Rossetti says that 'to walk in Christ's incomparable footsteps is both easy and difficult', that is the Christian goal:

> There waits in every direction abundant good to be done, if only we have the will patiently to do it, first counting the cost. For though no literal mountain obstruct our path, mountainous opposition may confront us; and if it please not God to remove it, then in His strength, weary and heartsore as we may be, we must surmount it, 'looking unto Jesus'.[29]

Rossetti turns the selfishness of the age on its head: 'To whom does a man give himself? To one whom he loves as himself. Such is the standard of human self-gift; and Christ, Very Man no less than Very God, will not fall short of it. To "the friend that is as His own soul" will He give Himself; giving Himself, He will withhold nothing'.[30]

The materiality of Rossetti's theology manifests through several strains. Apart from the materialist theology of bodily resurrection infusing her belief in the importance of caring for the bodies as well as the souls of her community – that is, the Communion of Saints – fasting is also a material, ethical act as much as it is an act of spiritual edification. Furthermore, her awareness of the materiality allows her to use poetry, like many other High Anglican theologians, to infuse her theology, bringing together the spiritual and the corporeal, as much as the Real Presence doctrine of the Eucharist inexplicably fuses together the divine and the human. The poetry in Rossetti's theological works becomes a literary form of fasting. This kind of fasting provides succinct punctuation and condensation of thought. Fasting and poetic structure work similarly to contain both emotional and spiritual excess, which directs the focus outward. Rossetti's participation in High Church liturgy, her religious impulses and her adherence to the Doctrine of Reserve are strongly connected, both spiritually and aesthetically, to her pragmatism in fighting for social justice. Fasting was a way of ethically entering into an understanding of eating only what the body needs, rather than an excess, and then from that position moving into active work in the community to help the vulnerable. Throughout her theological works, Rossetti engages with fasting, not only as a spiritual discipline, but as a physical discipline that builds resilience for times of scarcity and alerts the mind via the stomach to one's responsibility to provide for the poor, a central tenet of Christian duty.

Unity of the body

> Christ, our Judge and our only Saviour, keep us from being numbered amongst those who, standing on the left hand at the bar of judgment, shall make answer, 'Lord, when saw we Thee?'
> (St. Matt. xxv. 41, 44)[31]

Rossetti concludes *Seek and Find* (1879) with a prayer that she and her readers alike would learn to recognize Christ in the vulnerable. The parable she references is significant because in it Christ speaks to his disciples about providing for the protection, nourishment and health of the least significant members of the community. To serve them is to serve Christ, and their physical health is to be valued because their bodies are archetypes of the Body of Christ. Recognizing that the vulnerable are as much a part of the Body of Christ as the privileged extends into the growing discourse in the nineteenth century of the social body, with the conviction that the failure of health in any part of that body has an impact on the entirety. Throughout her theological works, Rossetti challenges the unhealthy excesses of the rich as both disabling the poor further and harming themselves. She encourages an ethical reassessment of need, want and hunger that stands against the impetus of individualism, greed and gluttony. In *Letter and Spirit* she writes: 'Our bodily needs and infirmities will be sanctified if they become to us a parable of spiritual significance; for they are not even in their own nature blameworthy while curbed and directed aright'.[32] It is not wrong to feel the pull of appetite, but appetite needs to be subject to reason and justice – that is, considered with spiritual significance. Indeed, the joy and pleasure of appetite can only be fully experienced if it is connected to the sacramental understanding of the individual body's connection to nature, and its part within the sacred Body of Christ.

In *Letter and Spirit*, Rossetti likens the interconnectedness of the social body to that of the Trinity. In exploring fellow-feeling and the Divine Unity, she argues that if in 'every aspect of creation there must exist the corresponding Divine Archetype', then conversely, there must be a representation in creation of the Trinity.[33] Interestingly, a similar analogy was used to argue for the joining of the Three Branches of Anglicanism, Roman Catholicism and Eastern Orthodoxy. In this context, however, Rossetti is referring to the unity of the Body of Christ, the Community of Saints and the social body. All three representations are of interdependent community with varying degrees of temporal and eternal significance, but all are pertinent to Rossetti's perspective. She writes, '[E]ven as our God is One, so does He summon us to become one in His service', calling her reader to recognize their oneness with the rest of humanity as a divine ordination.[34] It is from this position of oneness that she challenges the 'disinclination' within society to serve one another with a generous spirit. 'Far from breaking with Mary', she writes, 'we eke out our spikenard, and, unlike the Apostles, are more intent on rescuing the last fragments than on spreading the feast'.[35]

It is significant that Rossetti connects and inverts the biblical accounts of Mary the forgiven sinner who anoints Christ's feet with expensive oils, much to the chagrin of Judas, and the feeding of the five thousand. These two examples of divine generosity are brought together as parallels: the five thousand are also the Body of Christ, which was anointed by Mary's oils – they may even be the feet, a less pleasant part of the body – but further, Rossetti observes that her society is more likely to side with Judas, and attempt to horde the remains following the feast, forgetting the act of abundant generosity that preceded it. To feed the poor is to feed Christ; to nourish them is to anoint Christ's Body. Furthermore, ministering to one part of the Body ministers to the whole. The 'sin of Disinclination'[36] to which Rossetti repeatedly refers not only leads to social chaos but reflects a disinclination to serve God that causes an unhealthy disunity in the Body.

Like Robert Evans, Rossetti sees active service as the evidence of godliness; yet she disagrees with him on fasting as she sees the dual act of prayer and fasting as a means of promoting the necessary empathy for the poor to perform such active service with integrity. In *The Face of the Deep* (1893), she writes: 'Nothing on earth is a substitute for the performance of duty... "Is any among you afflicted? let him pray,"' adding, 'prayer being practical and PROMOTIVE OF PRACTICE.'[37] Prayer is not the end but the means to action. For Rossetti, fasting teaches the faster to curb 'self-indulgence and personal luxuries,'[38] and to be like Christ, who will 'give Himself; giving Himself, He will withhold nothing.'[39] Even more pertinently, she observes 'Christ is Head of the Church: should a martyred Head have a pampered body?'[40] Rossetti is not talking about self-abnegation; what she rejects is pampering and luxury – excesses – not the consumption of what the body needs in order to be strong and healthy. Her challenge is toward selfish excess and gluttony in this instance, yet she also rejects the self-indulgence of excessive restraint that debilitates body and mind. Any kind of excess, whether of indulgence or restraint, leads to self-centredness. Rossetti's purpose is toward seeing Christ instead of self, which includes seeing Christ in others, especially those in need.

Within Rossetti's theology of fasting and consumption lies the paradox of being simultaneously satisfied and insatiable, a state that reflects an awareness of being complete in being one with nature (God's creation), the mortal life being but a shadow of the afterlife, where true fullness will be known. One should be satisfied with God's goodness and provision on the earth, but at the same time not satisfied to the point of glorying in the earthly instead of in the promise of the Divine. Restrained consumption is tied to faith in God's provision on earth as well as in the life to come and fidelity to Christ's command to feed and clothe the poor, hungry and vulnerable. In *Seek and Find* Rossetti writes:

> Beauty essential is the archetype of imparted beauty; Life essential, of imparted life; Goodness essential, of imparted goodness: but such objects, good, living, beautiful, as we now behold, are not that very Goodness, Life, Beauty, which (please God) we shall one day contemplate in beatific vision. Then shall fully come to pass that saying: 'They that eat me shall yet be hungry, and they that drink me shall yet be thirsty' (Ecclus. xxiv. 21); only with a hunger and thirst which shall abide at once satisfied and insatiable. Then, not now: now let us turn to a spiritual signification the prayer of Agur: 'Remove far from me vanity and lies: give me neither poverty nor riches; feed me with food convenient for me' (Prov. xxx. 8). If even St. Paul might have been exalted above measure through abundance of revelation (2 Cor. xii. 7), let us thank God that we in our present frailty know not any more than His Wisdom reveals to us: not that man's safety resides in ignorance any more than in knowledge, but in conformity of the human to the divine will. See the Parable of the Talents, St. Luke xix. 12-26; where the sentence depends on the fidelity of the servants, rather than in the amount of the trust.[41]

After putting earthly beauty and provision in its rightful place as an archetype of the heavenly, she puts this contemplation in the context of the apocryphal invitation of Wisdom in Ecclesiasticus:

> Come unto me, all ye that be desirous of me, and fill yourselves with my fruits. For my memorial is sweeter than honey, and mine inheritance than the honeycomb. They that eat me shall yet be hungry, and they that drink me shall yet be thirsty. He that obeyeth

me shall never be confounded, and they that work by me shall not do amiss.⁴²

As much as one realizes with wisdom the little one can know, one must consume with the knowledge that one cannot be fully satisfied on the earth and should not try to consume as if seeking satisfaction.

As Rossetti refers to the prayer of Agur in the Book of Proverbs, the aim for moderation is reinforced: 'give me neither poverty nor riches; feed me with the food convenient for me'. Significantly, the English Standard Bible (ESV) translates the final phrase as 'the food that is needful for me'. This concept is pertinent to Rossetti's High Anglican theology of consumption. Yet even in the translation Rossetti uses, there is a compulsion further into an understanding of one's connection to creation: food that is convenient could refer to that which is seasonal, local or simple – in contrast to the imperial compulsion in nineteenth-century Britain to partake in all the delicacies and wonders plundered from around the globe onto Britain's shores. The verse following the one that Rossetti cites explains, 'Lest I be full, and deny thee, and say, Who is the Lord? or lest I be poor, and steal, and take the name of my God in vain'.⁴³ Within Rossetti's call for individual moderation, there is not only an outward view to society and social issues, but an even broader scope into the spirit of the imperial age. A glutted body becomes sluggish and indolent, as much as a starving one is made weak. In contrast to the social body that seeks more and more to consume – luxuries, excesses, the exotic – the Body of Christ is a fasted body: one that is not wasted, but also is not overly filled. Its moderation makes it both strong and healthy.

Liturgical practice

As the Orthodox theologian Alexander Schmemann notes, the purpose of the liturgy 'is not the individual sanctification of its members, but the creation of the people of God as the Body of Christ'.[44] Liturgical practice, then, is what forms the understanding of the Body of Christ. As much as there is an imperative in Rossetti's theology of fasting to recognize one's connection both to creation and to the Body of Christ, and therefore to consume in a sacramental way, that idea of sacrament can never be separated from the imperative to provide materially for the poor. In *The Face of the Deep*, Rossetti embeds the poem 'Because He first loved us' within her comments on fasting, emphasizing that God's provision is given with a command to use such provision to provide for others:

> I was hungry, and Thou feddest me;
>   Yea, Thou gavest drink to slake my thirst:
> O Lord, what love gift can I offer Thee
>   Who hast loved me first? –
>
> Feed My hungry brethren for My sake;
>   Give them drink, for love of them and Me:
> Love them as I loved thee, when Bread I brake
>   In pure love of thee. –
>
> Yea, Lord, I will serve them by Thy grace;
>   Love Thee, seek Thee, in them; wait and pray:
> Yet would I love Thyself, Lord, face to face,
>   Heart to heart, one day. –
>
> Let to-day fulfil its daily task,
>   Fill thy heart and hand to them and Me:
> To-morrow thou shalt ask, and shalt not ask
>   Half I keep for thee.[45]

The placement of the poem reinforces the social, outward focus of fasting, as well as the motive of disciplining the one who fasts to trust in God's provision – a daily provision, like the manna from heaven, that resists hoarding and excess. The alternation of the stanzas as a conversation between Christ and a devout mimics the call and response within the Mass; yet the distinction of parts is blurred through the devotee using Christ's words – 'I was hungry, and Thou feddest me'. This is a reversal of Matthew 25:40, 'Inasmuch as ye have done it unto one of the least of these my brethren, ye have done it unto me'. The position of the poem, then, starts with the assumption of God's provision; and from that position, there is an expectation on the Church subsequently to be Christ and provide for those who do not have – to feed the hungry brethren for Christ's sake.

The poem is immediately followed, however, by the ironic maxim 'God accepts dues as gifts. Man receives gifts as dues', and then Rossetti goes on to say,

> An eminent physician once told me that there are people who would benefit in health by fasting: a secondary motive, yet surely not an unlawful one. To perform a duty from a motive which is not wrong, may prove a step towards performing it from the motive which is right. To leave it unperformed seems the last contrivance adapted to result in its performance.[46]

Rossetti confronts the attitude of selfishness and imperialist entitlement in society through the maxim yet attempts to encourage fasting as something that is good for oneself as well as others, in the hope that through performing the act, right motives may develop. In *Letter and Spirit*, Rossetti's exegesis on the Ten Commandments, the connections between right motives, social justice and individual restraint are brought together in terms of idolatry. Idolatry is not merely a theological concept of spiritual worship, but idolatrous acts are shown to have material impact on the function (and dysfunction) of human society.

Rossetti argues that 'breaches' of the Commandments 'strike at the root of human society and tend towards the bringing on of social chaos'.[47] All of the Commandments come under the transgression of idolatry, and all idolatry is a form of putting oneself before God and neighbour:

> The idolater substitutes in his heart and worship something material in lieu of God; and as being material, akin to himself and unlike God: the murderer, the sensualist, the thief, substitutes for his neighbour or for the well-being of that neighbour some personal indulgence or acquisition of his own: *each postpones God or man to self.*[48]

Idolatry is remedied in Rossetti's theology by actively curbing one's appetite for indulgence and excess. Importantly, Rossetti argues that the Seventh Commandment, regarding adultery, is analogous to the alimentary appetites, thus 'forbid[ding]… the over-indulgence of any bodily appetite'.[49] She continues with an argument of fasting tied with giving to the poor as a remedy for this sin: 'thus, gluttony and drunkenness range under this Commandment: moreover, experience teaches us that such gross gratifications, and even that wealth, ease, luxury, unchastened by almsgiving and self-denial, pre-dispose frail humankind towards further excesses'.[50]

Rossetti acknowledges the challenge of restraining one's appetites through the biblical example of Esau, who, 'harassed by hunger, bartered for food his irrecoverable birthright'.[51] In terms of perspective, the biblical account says that Esau was hungry from a day's work, not due to famine or starvation. Thus Rossetti sees him as one who prioritizes his temporal physical appetite over things that remain. Yet while citing the hard proverb 'Put a knife to thy throat, if thou be a man given to appetite',[52] she also acknowledges the struggle not to focus on the physical appetites or allow them to rule decision-making: 'Yet hunger and thirst we must here perforce in body and soul, and hope and long with unsatisfied cravings'. She adds from the Beatitudes, 'Blessed are they that hunger and thirst for righteousness: for they shall be filled', but even in her acknowledgement of the necessity for hunger and thirst, there remains both a need to give it purpose and to moderate it so that one does not give into the temptation of Esau. The answer is found in liturgical practice:

> Our bodily needs and infirmities will be sanctified if they become to us a parable of spiritual significance; for they are not even in their own nature blameworthy while curbed and directed aright... And while Christ bids us hunger and thirst after righteousness, let us not forget that He Himself is the Righteousness for which He bids us crave.[53]

Rossetti therefore suggests that there was nothing wrong with Esau's hunger, but in his elevation of that hunger over more eternal matters. Fasting recognizes the temporality of the mortal world, as well as embracing the state of hunger that the world is for many, both spiritually and physically. To indulge in excess and gluttony is not only to deny the suffering of others, but to defy the satisfaction of heaven. The way to bring physical needs into spiritual significance is to incorporate them into liturgical practice: not just in the Sunday Masses, but through the entirety of the liturgical calendar of fasts, feasts and remembrances. As Rossetti notes, 'He who will not exercise so much self-discipline as to map out his six days with tolerable accuracy, is the last man to draw an unswerving line of sacred demarcation around the seventh day'[54]

Regular corporate fasting – that is, shared fasting according to the liturgical calendar – prepares the community for times of scarcity, but it is also meant to remind the fasters of their responsibility to each other, as well as the disbalances of human society in contrast to the justice of Providence. In her reading of Revelations 6:5-6 in *The Face of the Deep*, Rossetti nuances the representation of famine in the image of the pair of balances in the hand of the rider of the black horse in a way that acknowledges that the state of famine is not the state of there not *being* enough, but of some individuals, or some sections of society, not having access to, or command of, enough. Rossetti writes: 'Famine: yet not absolute foodlessness: else, why the pair of balances?'[55] She draws out the added horror, not just of lack, but of some having while others who do not have look on in hunger. She then goes on to say,

> The balances suggest scarcity short of literal nullity: hunger, but not necessarily starvation. Scarcity imposes frugality, exactness; a gathering up of fragments, with thanksgiving because there remain fragments to gather. No waste, latitude, margin; no self-pampering can be tolerated, but only a sustained self-denial: self must be stinted, selfishness starved, to give to him that needeth.[56]

Rossetti draws attention to the fact that during many times of famine there is food present, and therefore starvation is not necessary. She implies that through being willing to sacrifice a portion of one's own privilege, others in the community should not have to suffer from hunger: it is better for all to have some than for some to have all.

Anglican liturgical practice is designed to reinforce the Communion of the Saints, both as one family in heaven and earth, and across the Church on earth. Therefore, if some are starving, it should affect all. The reference to gathering up of fragments is yet another allusion to Christ feeding the five thousand and, given that the Church is meant to be Christ's body on earth, it is the responsibility of the Church to gather up their own fragments to give to those in need. This is a particularly pertinent reference, given the prevalence of food wastage in Rossetti's London. The rhythms of the liturgical calendar are brought into play as Rossetti adds: 'as the poor never cease out of the land and are in various degrees standing representatives of famine, this self-stinting seems after all to be the rule and standard of right living; not a desperate exceptional resource, but a regular, continual, plain duty'.[57] While it is comparatively easier to give to the suffering at the moment of acute crisis, it is much harder to give continually to the chronically suffering. The need for a continual resource requires the moderation and regularity of liturgical practice: the rhythms of the weeks and months give order to the duties of the participant, in both their fasting and their giving, externalizing the pressures of expectation.

Within the context of liturgical practice lies Rossetti's Orthodox theological understanding of a Lenten life, as expressed through her Lenten poems. In particular, 'Mid-Lent' reveals Rossetti's resonance with Orthodox theology. While Roman Catholicism practices Lent in the forty days leading to Easter, Orthodoxy practices four extended fasting periods throughout the liturgical calendar. The one preceding Easter is called 'Great Lent', while the time known as Advent, leading to Christmas, in the Roman Church, is called 'Lent' in the Eastern Church. Rossetti's 'Mid-Lent' was originally published without title as the entry for December 9 in *Time Flies* (1886),[58] and therefore at the beginning of the middle week of the Orthodox Lent. Rossetti later included it in *Verses* (1893) in the section of poems under 'Feasts and Fasts'. Her adherence to the Orthodox liturgy of fasting lends her theology to the idea that fasting is to be a constant practice throughout the seasons of the year. It is further evident that she sought to regulate the motive of fasting within the liturgical structure. In its original publication, she provides no commentary on the poem; the verses alone are meant to speak to the reader:

> Is any grieved or tired? Yea, by God's Will:
>   Surely God's Will alone is good and best:
>   O weary man, in weariness take rest,
> O hungry man, by hunger feast thy fill.
> Discern thy good beneath a mask of ill,
>   Or build of loneliness thy secret nest:
>   At noon take heart, being mindful of the west,
> At night wake hope, for dawn advances still.
> At night wake hope. Poor soul, in such sore need
>   Of wakening and of girding up anew,
>   Hast thou that hope which fainting doth pursue?
> No saint but hath pursued and hath been faint;
> Bid love wake hope, for both thy steps shall speed,
>   Still faint yet still pursuing, O thou saint.[59]

Rossetti acknowledges the weariness associated with hunger, but uses irony to moderate the self-focus, encouraging the faster not to focus on themselves in that moment. The poem can be read in terms of spiritual nourishment through physical self-denial, but in the context of Rossetti's theological prose, it can also be read as wanting the reader to have some perspective in relation to their own privilege, and to rethink what they consider weariness or hunger in comparison to those in dire want, as opposed to those who choose to fast – as, perhaps, Esau might have done. The suggestion to 'Discern the good beneath the ill' can be read as one's own spiritual development, but Rossetti is also asking her readers to consider the good they are doing others through their self-sacrifice. The outward, community focus is made evident in the 'Or' of 'Or build of loneliness thy secret nest'. Yes, fasting is meant to be done in secret – that is, privately – but it does not have to be lonely. The alternative to having an outward focus in fasting is to be isolated from the community through a spiritual self-interest of the kind that Robert Evans abhorred. Rather, Rossetti suggests that fasting should be done 'being mindful of the west'. This reference relates to the positioning of the altar in the church. There was a debate about whether priests should face away from the congregation – toward the altar, thereby facing the east – or if they should stand behind the altar, thus facing the congregation and the west. In Rossetti's poem, strength for the fast must be found in facing the people, the Body of Christ, focusing on the community's needs as the reason to continue. It is that outward focus that enables one to 'At night wake hope' and be 'Still faint yet pursuing'.

Social prophecy

Rossetti's theology confronts human selfishness and fear with resilience determined by an outward purpose. The ethics of fasting are tied incontrovertibly to feeding the hungry, so the practice of fasting implies the practice of giving to the poor. As much as Rossetti maintained the practice of liturgical fasting, including charitable work and giving, her theological representations of fasting further elevate the material value of fasting as being as crucial as any spiritual benefit. Fasting is not just a spiritual practice, but a means to consume only what is necessary. It is a way of life, and Rossetti notably owned few clothes or other possessions and spent little apart from on food and rent.[60] Necessity itself was being redefined in industrial, imperial Britain in social, economic and political terms; and within these lenses, Rossetti adheres to the moderation first learned through the Anglican liturgy, enabling her to narrate a kind of fasting that is both ethical and spiritual, focused outward as well as upward, while practically benefitting the poor. True to the Anglican (and Orthodox) ethos, Rossetti's theology was practical: 'Works, we infer, preach at least as powerfully as words; and this form of sermon all can deliver, even those who have neither call nor eloquence as teachers'.[61] Yet it must be noted that such statements are not intended as evangelical in tone, but instead a prompting to the Body of Christ as it stands to respond to its call to minister to the earth. The purpose of social prophecy within Rossetti's theological works is not to convert the fallen, but to reform the professed faithful. 'Only we Christians', she writes,

> are beyond all others bound to keep in view that a vexatious petty scrupulousness forms no part of our Sunday duty, while works of mercy are never more holy than on that holy day... our hallowed rest is promoted and not violated by services of love done in the love of God to our brethren.[62]

Her social prophecy goes even deeper, calling for reform in England's governance and economic structures, to which she lends the divine weight of theological rhetoric.

As an extended commentary on the Book of Revelations, *The Face of the Deep* lends itself readily to overt social prophecy. Rossetti uses the visions of the apocalypse to convey her critique of the consumerism and excess of Britain, and the perverse gap between rich and poor. 'Alas England full of luxuries and thronged by stinted poor', she writes, 'whose merchants are princes and whose dealings crooked, whose packed storehouses stand amid bare homes, whose gorgeous array has rags for neighbours!'[63] She prays with bitter irony for the state of the nation: 'From a canker in our gold and silver, from a moth on our garments, from blasted crops, from dwindling substance, from righteous retribution abasing us among the nations, Good Lord, deliver us'.[64] Divine judgement is understood, then, as a levelling force, in which those who depend upon excesses are the ones who will be touched most by their removal and destruction. They are the ones who practice idolatry and are left shaken when the temporal is removed. Similarly, in *Letter and Spirit*, 'luxuries enhance the ensnaring influence of the world', and 'personal comforts are like locked-up capital bearing no interest'.[65] The remedy is a changed focus: 'The heart once divorced from earth, the things of earth dwindle to pettiness; we possess our souls in patience, and await that day when the righteous shall shine forth as the sun in the kingdom of their Father'.[66]

This changed focus is entirely consumed by ethics and social justice. Rossetti is not just concerned with giving, but how one gives. She posits that 'what we may lawfully clip, pare, stint, is our own provision; the unique person who we have a right to grind is ourself'; yet she goes on to add,

> A munificent giver must not be a fraudulent acquirer, or here niggardly and there lavish; or open-handed in response to calls upon generosity, while lax or evasive when justice puts in a claim. Even unselfish persons, if they permit themselves to be generous at the cost of justice, substitute the kind of luxury they relish for another kind which they care not for: generosity is *their* luxury; yet

if incompatible with justice it must be foregone. Charities in debt exhibit a dubious side as well as an edifying one; and if charities, how much more the common run of debtors.[67]

Yet what is even more noteworthy is Rossetti's willingness to combine economics with theology, directly engaging with the science of political economy that had, arguably, replaced God and Justice in nineteenth-century Britain with the similarly unearthly 'invisible hand' that was believed to regulate the market.

Like her Tractarian predecessors, Rossetti sees the value in economy in terms of God's economy, which she sets in opposition to the world's idea of economy:

> From the noble desire to give, springs that apparently alien and by comparison mean virtue, Economy: for no revenues, however vast, can be administered to advantage while sapped by waste. Economy is oftentimes a shamefaced virtue; more prone to blush when to keep clear of dishonesty poverty practices it by constraint, than when ample means are voluntarily husbanded for the sake of some unselfish purpose. On the contrary, when economy lapses into stinginess it frequently parades itself with brasen effrontery, visibly hugging itself and despising its betters.[68]

Building on the work done by early Tractarians, who frequently wrote on the growing impetus of political economy in nineteenth-century Britain, Rossetti critiques political economy in terms of ethical practice and as an excuse not to give. She sets up two kinds of economists: the sordid Economist and the heavenly minded Economist. Apart from the fact that she genders both as female, inserting women into a public sphere of action and responsibility that much of society would deny them, she also exposes that economy itself is not the problem, but rather the human motivations behind it. In fact, economy is necessary in Rossetti's theology: like early Tractarians, economizing is at the heart of moderation for her, and liturgical practice is about creating a pattern and framework for such economy. Being economical means resisting excess; there can be an excess of self-righteousness and judgement as much as there can be an excess of giving that would lead to further social chaos, not to mention potential bitterness and resentment on the part of the one who gives excessively, beyond their means and beyond what Rossetti would class as right motives.

Rossetti first presents the 'sordid Economist', who

> walks the world unabashed, and says her say complacently in company. She keenly realises and relishes the distinction between elevenpence three farthings and one shilling, and ignoring all claims of neighbourhood, however struggling and meritorious the neighbour, frequents remote shops in honour of this distinction. Her remarks turn on prices, and linger in the store-room or the coal-cellar. She gossips about the extravagance of this dinner-giver, and the wastefulness of that household, frittering away her own and her neighbour's time, not to speak of her neighbour's patience. To save a halfpenny she will squander time recklessly, that priceless, irrecoverable treasure time. Her tastes, aims, contemplations, standard, are of the earth, earthly.[69]

In contrast, the 'heavenly-minded Economist' is one who

> reflects how when our Lord bade 'Gather up the fragments that remain, that nothing be lost' (St. John vi. 5-13), it was after feeding a multitude to the full; therefore fragments become precious to her for her own consumption, because thus she can succour the larger number of her brethren, and yet more, because thus she imitates Christ. 'She... eateth not the bread of idleness;'... enabling herself the more abundantly to stretch out her hand to the poor, yea, both hands to the needy. Her diet approaches the dinner of herbs with love: her own dress is plainer than the letter of the apostolic injunction prescribes, 'not with gold, or pearls, or costly array;' yet may she find scarlet for her household, wine for her friends (*see* St. John ii. 1-11)... if ever the balance trembles doubtfully between

gift and thrift, her glad preference weights the scale of gift and sends thrift flying upward. All the same, she wastes nothing.[70]

For Rossetti, a life of restraint – a fasted life – integrates all aspects and motivation – from the use of time, to food, to rest, all as lived worship. The life of restraint is not motivated from a position of self-abnegation, but of conscious consumption that consumes no more nor less than is healthful. The way in which Rossetti juxtaposes the metaphor of the bread of idleness with the act of stretching her hands to the needy, followed by maintaining a dinner 'approaching' the dinner of herbs, but not reaching that point of self-denial, reveals a necessary tension of restraint that brings together all human acts within a narrow channel between excesses, propelled by faith in divine increase. If the heavenly economist errs, it is on the side of 'gift' rather than 'thrift'; for Rossetti not only challenges the motives of excess and gluttony, but a self-righteous withholding that is loosely veiled meanness. She is not frivolous in her giving, yet neither is she stingy.

As much as Rossetti uses the images of these two economists to challenge the spirit of her age, she also directly addresses England in biblical terms. England becomes the doomed, complacent Zion condemned by the prophet Amos:

The Prophet Amos (vi. 1-7) portrays a pampered ease-loving community, and foretells their doom: 'Woe to them that are at ease in Zion… Ye that put far away the evil day… That lie upon beds of ivory, and stretch themselves upon their couches, and eat the lambs out of the flock, and the calves out of the midst of the stall; that chant to the sound of the viol, and invent to themselves instruments of musick, like David; that drink wine in bowls, and anoint themselves with the chief ointments: but they are not grieved for the affliction of Joseph. Therefore now shall they go captive with the first that go captive, and the banquet of them that stretched themselves shall be removed;' words, which to us of the nineteenth century, and not least to us of England, speak with an awful omen.

> Surely for us, as for Nebuchadnezzar of old, it is high time to 'break off our sins by righteousness, and our iniquities by showing mercy to the poor; if it may be a lengthening of our tranquility'.[71]

Importantly, Rossetti is not speaking here to secular society, but to the Body of Christ: those who pride themselves in outward displays of ritual and worship, without recognizing the luxurious way they live as a form of gluttony, and do not see the requirement to show mercy to the poor – indeed, Rossetti speaks to the hypocritical irony of a church that displays pomp and wealth, while justifying lack of charity via the harshest interpretations of political economy, and a spirituality that believes that poverty is God's judgement on the unrighteous. It is a church that makes wealth their god, forgetting the poverty of Christ.

In Rossetti's materialist theology, fasting is tied to a considered restriction of all appetites – alimentary, labour, wealth and other commodities – and becomes the means by which an ethical position can be reached that will benefit the health and well-being not just of the individual who practices fasting, but of the whole community. As a social prophet, she both challenges society and seeks to bring her readers under the vision of seeing Christ in the hungry and vulnerable. In 'Surely He hath borne our griefs', a sonnet first published in *Verses* (1893), the volta occurs when the human faces turn from themselves to have compassion on those around them. They see Christ's face reflected in the faces of others, especially those who are less privileged:

> If grief be such a looking-glass as shows
>   Christ's Face and man's in some sort made alike,
>   Then grief is pleasure with a subtle taste:
>   Wherefore should any fret or faint or haste? (9-12)

'Man' in this sense is not just individual humans but all of humankind – that connection between the Trinity and the social body, individual humans a part of each other as much as Rossetti sees the three elements of the Trinity as one. A way, then, of reading 'Wherefore should any fret or faint or haste' could be a challenge to those who *have* – either sustenance or strength – to make sure that there is provision for other members of the same social body. The willingness to recognize this responsibility comes from the perspective of Christ's example: 'He hungered Who the hungry thousands fed' (7). Christ could empathize because he felt their hunger – had experienced hunger himself. That is what fasting is meant to do for humankind in Rossetti's view. Rossetti responds to those who, like Evans, saw fasting as 'righteousness overmuch': 'Is our most urgent temptation that which inclines us to do too much, or that which lulls us to do too little, or to do nothing?'[72] In this questioning, Rossetti aligns with many theologians and medical professionals who saw the need to resist gluttony and excess, along with their counterpart spirits of individualism and, in Rossetti's words, 'disinclination', as a much greater danger to the moral and physical health of Victorian society than the problem of consuming too little.

Notes

1. Robert Wilson Evans, *The Ministry of the Body* (London: Francis & John Rivington, 1847), 212–13.
2. Élie Halévy, *The Triumph of Reform: 1830–1841*. Trans. E. I. Watkin (New York: Barns & Noble, 1961), 145.
3. Evans, *Ministry of the Body*, 10.
4. Ibid., 12.
5. Ibid., 13–14.
6. Ibid., 9.
7. Ibid., 16–17.
8. In particular, see Emma Mason, 'Christina Rossetti and the Doctrine of Reserve', *Journal of Victorian Culture*, 7.2 (2002): 196–219 and Kirstie Blair, *Form and Faith in Victorian Poetry and Religion* (Oxford: Oxford University Press, 2012).

9. Elizabeth Ludlow, *Christina Rossetti and the Bible: Waiting with the Saints* (London: Bloomsbury, 2014), 24.
10. Ibid., 60.
11. Emma Mason, *Christina Rossetti: Poetry, Ecology, Faith* (Oxford: Oxford University Press, 2018), 57.
12. Ibid., 84, 9.
13. Ibid., 14.
14. Geoffrey Rowell, *The Vision Glorious: Themes and Personalities of the Catholic Revival in Anglicanism* (Oxford: Oxford University Press, 1991), 3–4.
15. Michelle Tusan, *Smyrna's Ashes: Humanitarianism, Genocide, and the Birth of the Middle East* (Berkeley: University of California Press, 2012), 3.
16. Graham Woolfenden, 'Eastern Christian Liturgical Traditions: Eastern Orthodox', in *The Blackwell Companion to Eastern Christianity*, ed. Ken Parry, 319–38 (London: Blackwell, 2007), 319.
17. Todd O. Williams, 'The Autobiographical Self and Embodied Knowledge of God in Christina Rossetti's *Time Flies*', *Literature and Theology*, 28.3 (2014): 321–33, 327.
18. George Moore, *The Power of the Soul over the Body, Considered in Relation to Health and Morals* (1845; New York: Harper & Brothers, 1847), 32.
19. Ibid., 190. Emphasis added.
20. Ibid., 241.
21. Anna Kyugovoy Silver, *Victorian Literature and the Anorexic Body* (Cambridge: Cambridge University Press, 2002), 139.
22. Christina Rossetti, *Seek and Find. A Double Series of Short Studies* (London: SPCK, 1879), 96–7.
23. Christina Rossetti, *Letter and Spirit. Notes on the Commandments* (London: SPCK, 1883), 33.
24. Ibid., 34.
25. Rev. 10:10.
26. Christina Rossetti, *The Face of the Deep: A Devotional Commentary on the Apocalypse* (2nd ed. London: SPCK, 1893), 142.

27　Rossetti, *Letter and Spirit*, 35.
28　Ibid.
29　Rossetti, *Face of the Deep*, 84.
30　Ibid., 84.
31　Rossetti, *Seek and Find*, 327.
32　Rossetti, *Letter and Spirit*, 110–11.
33　Ibid., 13.
34　Ibid.
35　Ibid., 27.
36　Ibid., 34.
37　Rossetti, *Face of the Deep*, 59. Emphasis orig.
38　Ibid., 142.
39　Ibid., 84.
40　Ibid., 210.
41　Rossetti, *Seek and Find*, 14–15.
42　Ecclesiasticus 24: 19-22. Rossetti later alludes again to this passage in regard to spiritual and intellectual wisdom: *Seek and Find*, 36.
43　Prov. 30:9.
44　Alexander Schmemann, *Introduction to Liturgical Theology* (Crestwood, NY: St Vladimir's Seminary Press, 1966), 107.
45　Rossetti, *Face of the Deep*, 202–3.
46　Ibid.
47　Rossetti, *Letter and Spirit*, 77–8.
48　Ibid., 78. Emphasis added.
49　Ibid., 106.
50　Ibid.
51　Ibid., 108.
52　Ibid., 110. Prov. 23:2.
53　Ibid., 110–11.
54　Ibid., 178.
55　Rossetti, *Face of the Deep*, 202.
56　Ibid.
57　Ibid.

58 Christina Rossetti, *Time Flies: A Reading Diary* (1886; London: SPCK, 1901), 236–7.
59 Ibid.
60 Mason, *Christina Rossetti*, 15.
61 Rossetti, *Letter and Spirit*, 150.
62 Ibid., 175.
63 Rossetti, *Face of the Deep*, 422.
64 Ibid.
65 Rossetti, *Letter and Spirit*, 119.
66 Ibid., 118–19.
67 Ibid., 119–20.
68 Ibid., 120.
69 Ibid., 121.
70 Ibid., 121–2.
71 Ibid., 107.
72 Rossetti, *Letter and Spirit*, 29.

Josephine Butler's hagiography as social prophecy

They will be very unpopular, these Seers, if they are faithful. Many of the humbler people will hear them gladly, but the world will not love them. Quite the contrary. Conventional morality does not like to be disturbed; the respectable as well as the disreputable prejudices of ages are hard to root up.
– Josephine Butler, *Prophets and Prophetesses*, 1897[1]

Although only included in the calendar from the late twentieth century, Josephine Butler, like Christina Rossetti, is honoured as a saint within the Anglican liturgical tradition.[2] Her position as an Anglican saint signifies the impact of her life and work theologically and spiritually, while identifying her as a social prophet whose active work for social justice was of divine ordination. Her writing was an extension of this calling: a written expression of what Helen Mathers calls Butler's 'vital motivation'.[3] In her introduction to *Woman's Work and Woman's Culture* (1869), Butler writes that 'with respect to the social direction of certain principles of Christianity, my appeal is to Christ, and to Him alone, not to any Church, or traditions, or Councils, or catechisms, nor yet even to an Apostle', centring her faith in her social vision.[4] She continues, 'I appeal to Christ, and to Him alone, as the fountain-head of those essential and eternal truths which it is our duty and our wisdom to apply to all the changing circumstances of human society'.[5] Her audaciously direct appeal to Christ resonates with the medieval saints of whom she writes; and she further takes a key theological stance by asserting the primacy of the gospels and Christ's actions over the Pauline texts, attributing much of the division within the church to the Apostle's works while unity is found in the works of Christ: 'I believe all His acts to have had a supreme and everlasting significance. The teaching of His great typical acts is not less profound than that of His words. His teaching was for all time; much of St. Paul's was for a given time'.[6]

Like Gaskell and Rossetti, Butler's theology is practical: Christ's acts and words promoted social justice. Her biblical exegeses and hagiographies are therefore written with the purpose of catalysing a spiritual and moral transformation that leads to social transformation on earth. Just as fasting is an act in which the transformation of the individual leads to a transformed attitude of action, Butler's writing is intended to be a shaping of society as much as a shaping of self. As Butler recreates and transforms her own identity through her writing, she seeks to transform her readers through a new understanding of the past, present and future. Rebecca Styler observes that in the 'erosion of the self-other binary' in life-writing, there has developed a 'recognition of the porous boundaries between the biographer and their subject', which she observes throughout Butler's biographical works.[7] This porosity, however, goes beyond the author and subject in Butler's vision to encompass her audience. For Butler life-writing is a form of self-creation, much as Janet Larson has discussed Butler's writing on Saint Catharine of Siena as a way to understand and navigate her own path of campaigning for social and political reform,[8] but it is also a prophetic text in which the act of reading is meant to recreate the reader. Within this context, there are two aspects that need to be developed further: first, that all Butler's biographical writing, whether of Saint Agnes or Saint Catharine, or of her father or husband, effectively operates as hagiography with the necessary moral and spiritual implications of such a text; and second, her own position as a saint-in-waiting, with her writing envisaged as the teachings of a saint. That is not to suggest that Butler elevated herself, but that her work has been understood in terms of that of a mystic, theologian and spiritual teacher, as much as she was a social activist. It is through this multifocal lens that she needs to be addressed in relation to fasting and restrained consumption as ethical practices. Like her saints, Butler addresses those who '[mistake] the traditions of a vitiated Church for the essential ethics of Christ',[9] and in this way she seeks to correct the misapprehensions of the Church and of her age as a fulfilment of her divine calling. Butler does not talk about her own fasting explicitly, but this is consistent with gospel teachings to participate in such actions privately: 'when thou fastest, anoint thine head, and wash thy face; that thou appear not unto men to fast, but unto thy Father which is in secret'.[10] However, one significant mention of fasting is found in her biography of her father:

> The Book of the Prophet Isaiah was a great favourite, and his love for such words as the following, which he often quoted, was an index of the complexions of his mind: 'Is not this the fast that I have chosen? To loose the bands of wickedness, to undo the heavy burdens, and to let the oppressed go free, and that ye break every yoke?'[11]

In this recollection, Butler establishes a direct connection between theology, religious practice and social justice: fasting, like other practices, must consciously and actively alleviate injustice.

Butler is known for her campaigns against the Contagious Diseases Acts, and for promoting women's sexual, political and social equality. Less specific focus has been given to the way she emphasized the problem of women's economic precarity, apart from in its connection to the so-called fallen women she championed. She began her active social work by bringing vulnerable women into her home, having them become a part of her family and helping them gain independence. In this way, her actions reflect a continuation of the ethos of the

Plymleys of Shrewsbury, but Butler took her sympathies further to an extraordinary inclusion. Her theology of consumption and justice, then, must be understood in relation to her sense of genuine sisterhood with these women, which, as Mathers observes, 'may have been unwelcome to many female rescue workers', but was critical in 'suggesting an equality, a family relationship... [that] enabled Butler, almost uniquely among women rescue workers, to identify herself completely with the "fallen" woman. She believed that before God she was no more, and no less, than the equal of the Magdalen'.[12] Like the medieval saints, who gave their lives for their divine calling, Butler's theology was thoroughly merged with action. As Jane Jordan succinctly notes, 'In her eyes, religion and social justice were one'.[13]

The social and political influence of a saint

As an Anglo-Catholic, Christina Rossetti fits more readily into the notion of sainthood, while Mathers, among other scholars, has noted that it is unusual for an evangelical protestant like Butler to be included in such a concept. It is more helpful, however, to understand Butler in the context of her eclectic spiritual heritage, which becomes most evident in her biographical writings on her father and husband. A saint needs to experience some form of exile. Rossetti had her family's heritage of political exile from Italy. Butler's family heritage included Huguenots driven out of France and the Quaker tradition, as well as more conventional Anglicanism. Saints necessarily stand outside institutional norms, and for Rossetti and Butler, whose prophetic work was aimed at both the established church and secular society, they needed to stand at a distance from the institutions.

Most importantly, however, the social prophet is required to have a voice that speaks out of tune with the perceived spirit of the age. Butler critiques the manner in which parties place their denominational allegiance above what she sees as the legitimate work of Christ. Like her husband, who 'became a canon of Winchester Cathedral... [while] retain[ing] a sense of affectionate detachment from the Church's institutions',[14] Butler maintained strong relationships across a range of denominations while not clearly aligning herself with a particular branch of the church. Whereas recent scholarship has attempted uncomfortably to align Butler with evangelicalism, it is narrowing to situate her within any specific movement or persuasion. Alison Milbank reaches the closest when she implicitly connects Butler to the Broad Church through her relationship to F. D. Maurice, the famed Broad Church theologian, while also connecting her theology to Maurice's socialism. Yet Milbank takes care not to tie Butler too closely: 'Her theological ideas often chime in... with those of F. D. Maurice, who was well-known to her, and sometimes her social ideas are similar to those of certain Owenite socialists... it is worth noting that Maurice took many of his notions of socialism from the Owenites'.[15] Butler's sympathies with socialism link her to both Alice Meynell, who was an overt Christian Socialist, and Elizabeth Gaskell, who also claimed friendship with Maurice and was influenced by his socialism. Milbank defines Butler as a prophet and a mystic who finds inner authority, rather than outward authority through social institutions, and argues that in this manner she 'links the private and the social spheres without having the need to accept the terms of the latter. Indeed, prophecy is the expression of mysticism in practice'.[16] Whereas Milbank describes Butler as having 'personal' authority rather than institutional, it is more significant that from Butler's perspective, her authority was directly from the divine. The authority that Butler invoked was not dependent either on the established church in any form, or on social convention. Jenny Daggers and Diana Neal refer to Butler's conviction in her 'great gift of communion with God' as her 'prophetic consciousness', which flows into her theology, action and social vision.[17]

Thus Butler, as mystic, prophet and theologian, positions herself as possessing a divine authority and mandate to challenge the modern world, from its idolatrous relationship with capital to its unjust structures that punish the vulnerable and poor, especially women. She indirectly writes herself in hagiographic terms, particularly through her biography of her father, John Grey:

> My mother's parents were good people, descended from the poor but honest families of silk-weavers, driven out of France by the revocation of the Edict of Nantes. They were in the habit of opening their hospitable doors to everyone in the form of a religious teacher, of whatever sect, who happened to pass that way.[18]

Even on the most superficial level, the language is resonant with hagiography: the saint is descended from humble human lives and is familiar with both tribulation and being willing to give generously to strangers, despite their own poverty. However, this is not a medieval saint of whom Butler writes, but her own father, which means that she herself has descended from this heritage. She also draws close attention to her parents' attitude toward generous giving and including the vulnerable in their family as a marker for her own value in this regard. While writing her father as a saint, she is also revealing the deep influence he had on her own moral, theological and social visions:

> I believe that his political principles and public actions were alike the direct fruit of that which held rule within his soul – I mean his large benevolence, his tender compassionateness, and his respect for the rights and liberties of the individual man. His life was a sustained effort for the good of others, flowing from these affections. He had no grudge against rank or wealth, no restless desire to change for its own sake, still less any rude love of demolition; but he could not endure to see oppression or wrong of any kind inflicted on man, woman, or child... In the cause of any maltreated or neglected creature he was uncompromising to the last, and when brought

into opposition with the perpetrators of any social injustice he became an enemy to be feared... Yet the force which his hearers acknowledged lay in his love of truth, his clearness of judgement, and the known innocency of his life, rather than in rhetoric. The true key to an occasional bitterness against those whom he thought wrong-doers lay also in his great sensitiveness to wrong done. There was no self-satisfaction in his denunciation of evil; the contemplation of cruelty in any form was intolerable to him. He would speak of the imposition of social disabilities of any kind, by one class of persons on another, with kindling eyes and breath which came quickly; but he always turned away with a sense of relief from the subject of the evil-doers, or the evil done, to the persons who suffered, whose position his compassionate instinct would set him at once to the task of ameliorating.[19]

John Grey is positioned as a Christ-like or saint-like figure whose political and moral convictions coalesce with integrity and are outworked through public action with no selfish intent: 'His life was a sustained effort for the good of others'. His moral integrity is epitomized in his uncompromising inability to endure the oppression of the vulnerable alongside not being able to tolerate 'the contemplation of cruelty'. His prophetic voice is signalled through his 'kindling eyes and breath which came quickly', a voice inherited by his prophetic daughter who also 'became an enemy to be feared' in the face of social injustice.

Lucretia Flammang observes that 'where traditional theology failed Butler, she employed an alternative theology, drawn from her own feminist interpretations of the Bible'.[20] This alternative theology, while taught in part by the example of her father, was also learned through trying to reconcile lived experience with her understanding of a compassionate, just God. Jane Jordan writes of Butler's visit to Ireland in 1847 and the intense pain of the memory she held of the starving peasantry. Jordan infers that it was so painful for Butler that she suppressed the memory until 1887 when she wrote a pamphlet in support of Irish Home Rule. Importantly Jordan suggests that it was unlikely that Butler 'had witnessed acute distress amongst the poor until she came to Ireland. She said herself that there was no real poverty amongst the cottagers at Milfield or Dilston. What she saw in Ireland would remain with her for life'.[21] Jordan argues that it was through this experience, and being willing to grapple with the discomfort of it, that Butler was moved to take up 'what she saw as a divine call', that is, 'the cause of poor women', and

> to defend the seemingly indefensible: to identify herself with, and speak for, women who were regarded as the sewers of society… Her own approach to rescue work was highly unconventional. She began by taking prostitutes into her own family home, and regarded them as victims of social and economic circumstances rather than as guilty women.[22]

Butler's attitude in these actions is crucial: she 'offered food, shelter and tender nursing, as well as training and employment. She never spoke to them of their sin, never asked them about their past life, but instead offered them the possibility of a new life'.[23] She did not judge them for what some would consider sin but saw them as equals who had been disadvantaged through the unjust mechanisms of human society. It was her mission, not to convert the fallen, but to ameliorate the injustices. As Flammang pointedly observes, 'Butler believed that when she acted on behalf of prostitutes, she was obeying the will of God'.[24] Furthermore, in Butler's theology, rather than prostitution being the sin of fallen women, it is revisioned as the result of society's 'egregious departure from God's will that women and men be equal, that women as well as men are created for freedom from the oppression of others'. Flammang suggests that it was John Grey's abolition work that taught Butler 'to be sensitive to how people developed relationships of power over others. She recognized then that enslaved women had a unique set of horrors visited upon them'.²⁵ Indeed, Butler was able to adopt abolitionist narratives in her campaigns, arguing for the shared liberty of all regardless of gender or class, and acknowledging the economic and social power structures that worked against such liberty.

Butler's eclectic spirituality intersects with Katherine Plymley's evangelicalism almost 100 years earlier. Gleadle writes that

> the implications of the moral economy for personal consumption accorded well with the amalgamation of Evangelicalism and radical politics that already typified [Plymley's] views. In 1792 her personal notes on the Scriptures included a disquisition on what she perceived to be the shocking waste of food in elite households, noting that 'those whose fortune enables them to keep such a table' should realize it is 'an encroachment on the rights of the poor'.²⁶

Plymley was influenced by William Paley's concept of 'virtuous self-restraint' in his *Principles of Moral and Political Philosophy* (1785), although Gleadle notes that she was 'appalled to hear stories of Paley's apparent gluttony'. However, the crucial element in Plymley's attitude is the way in which she 'sought to establish [her] economic actions with reference to a specifical Anglican intellectual canon', one which emphasized the virtues of self-restraint in order to provide immediate relief to the disenfranchised.²⁷ As noted earlier, the Plymleys were a part of a wider social movement of 'dietary economy' in which wealthier members of the community focused on restricting their own household consumption in order 'to free up foodstuffs for the poor'.²⁸ It is interesting to note that Gleadle suggests that 'Consumption and cooking were, in this context, gendered as masculine concerns, related to the male-dominated worlds of high politics and public duties'. She continues:

> magistrates attempted to encourage 'the more fortunate in the virtues of self-sacrifice and restraint' as a means of assuaging the mounting food crisis. Joseph Plymley exemplified this pattern…

Joseph also took the lead in his household's consumption decisions, his domestic authority presumably bolstered by his masculine identities as a magistrate and an agricultural expert. 'My brother,' wrote Katherine Plymley, 'from a liberality of mind, has an utter repugnance to limit his servants in the articles of meat and drink, but as far as our own example went we spared bread as much as we easily could'.[29]

The example of the Plymleys, although significantly pre-dating Butler, provides a powerful heritage for Butler's own moral economy, with the exception that while the Plymleys maintained a feudal mindset of class position, Butler adopted a significantly more egalitarian perspective. Nevertheless, the desire to restrict waste and to make room for the sustenance of the poor – that is, attempting an equality of nourishment within all levels of society – is at the foreground of both visions. Butler writes in her introduction to *Woman's Work and Woman's Culture*, 'wherever there is monopoly on one hand, there is loss and waste on the other'.[30]

Butler's introduction to *Woman's Work and Woman's Culture* can be read as a theologico-economic treatise in which she calls for the privileged to redress the imbalances in society that unjustly punish the vulnerable. She appropriates her father's dislike of confronting uncomfortable truths of privilege, but 'believe[s] that there is no truer kindness than to remind those who, themselves just, true, and generous, have been born to an inheritance of monopolized privileges, of the duties which such an inheritance entails'.[31] Rather than allowing such 'evils in society' to be passed off as 'the result of accident', Butler calls to account those who do not take responsibility for what they have inherited, which includes the care of tenants and labourers:

> A man born to the possession of a great neglected estate, on which he finds his labourers degraded, cottages in ruins, and fields which ought to be storehouses of sustenance for city populations going to waste, undrained, and untilled, will scarcely think he has done

his duty to society if, having any available means of improving it, he dies, leaving his estate as he found it, content to charge the ruin and neglect upon his forefathers or upon a series of accidents. It would not be thought that an unjust accusation had been brought against such a landowner, if a friend were to take him by the hand, and lead him through the dwellings of his tenants and labourers, and bid him mark the moral as well as material harvest of misery which each year of continued neglect was preparing for a number of human beings; even if such a friend were to reason with him on 'righteousness, temperance, and judgment to come,' until he trembled in the waking sense of deep responsibility, it would not be thought to be a harsh or needless counsel.[32]

Butler seeks to bring the privileged alongside as perhaps ignorant rather than cruel; however, she also goes on to challenge the lack of moral health that leads to selfish enjoyment to the detriment of others. She suggests there 'is a moral deterioration which is the invariable attendant upon the habit of the careless and irresponsible enjoyment of possession at the expense of the happiness and good of others'. She adds, 'there is no certain moral health save in the awakened perception of the existing wrong, and the conscious will to restore the balance to society'.[33] The economic treatise turns to the theological as Butler continues:

In the Bible, I find the labourer deprived of just wages, the wronged widow, the neglected orphan, the leper driven out of society, the uninstructed from whom the key of knowledge had been withheld, the Gentile stranger oppressed by the privileged Jew, each and all in their turn tenderly mentioned in those pathetic and paternal utterances, beginning with 'Thus saith the Lord.' Their cry, it is said, enters into the ears of God. They are cared for by Him, and we dimly trust that restitution awaits them somewhere hereafter for loss suffered on earth.[34]

Butler's theological rhetoric is invested in mitigating responsibility for seemingly immoral actions performed by vulnerable individuals by attributing it to the unjust structures of an immoral society. For example, when she challenges the established doctrines regarding suicide, rather than framing it as the unforgivable sin that denies the victim burial in church grounds, Butler speaks with compassion of those 'maddened by life's mystery' who have 'voluntarily plunged into darkness' as rousing the pity of a God 'whose love and justice the poor heart can discern no longer athwart the black cloud of earth's cruelty'. The moral blame is turned upon those who benefit from and perpetuate the unjust system of privilege that leads to such despair: 'Yet I maintain that this very despair is less of a moral poison affecting the eternal destiny of a human spirit than is that blind self-satisfaction… which is engendered by the monopoly of privilege'.[35] Butler evokes a powerful image of excessive consumption by those 'who have rested in their privileges' as 'dream[ing] away their lives in a thraldom to conventions and customs which are *eating the heart out of society*'. It is in this image of unjust, violent consumption that Butler begins to assert her role as social prophet, invoking the 'language of the prophets speaking in God's name'.[36]

As a prophet, Butler calls upon her privileged readers to change their wasteful behaviours and actively seek to alleviate the suffering of others. Writing of the most recent census in 1861, she notes that while listing how many women were working for subsistence, it did not acknowledge the number who were working for 'starvation wages, nor how many of them have declined from a position of respectability to which they were born to one in any class or rank, however low, in which they may have a chance of earning a piece of bread'. She ironically refers to these 'breadwinners', and includes amongst them the 'armies of women' engaged in prostitution 'through the shutting up of avenues to a livelihood by means of trade monopolies among men'.[37] Her argument for expanding the possibilities for women's employment is apocalyptic: 'It has been said that nothing short of hunger will drive a nation to rebellion; but here we actually have a large measure of that ghastly element of rebellion – hunger and a lack of honestly-won food'.[38] Thus those who are privileged are challenged to rethink their moral assumptions regarding the poor, as well as their assumptions about those who assist them, while rhetorically empowering the vulnerable as an army. She argues that rather than the dismissive stereotype of the 'fervent advocates of woman's cause' being those 'who have been pinched and starved in the matter of affection, disappointed in life, embittered by isolation', there are many, in fact, who might have 'rested content, and more than content, with the sunshine which has fallen upon their path' if it were not for God not 'permit[ing] such a hardening of the heart'. Rather, Butler argues, 'it is precisely this abundance of blessing bestowed on them which urges them to care for the less happy, and which becomes a weight hardly to be born in the presence of the unloved'.[39] Like the call of the saint who gives up a comfortable life in service of the divine, Butler thus raises the prophetic challenge to rise above the comforts of one's own privilege, and, indeed, sacrifice some of that privilege for the sake of others:

> To be very patient under the miseries of *others*, appeared to us, as we grew up to years of discretion, to be an easy virtue: we desired to practise some sterner virtue than this, and we saw that our own happiness was the very reason why we should speak out boldly for the unhappy.[40]

Catharine of Siena's anorexic space

While Butler's language in discussing women's advocates is hagiographic, her more conventional hagiography of Catharine of Siena uses the historical figure of a medieval saint to provoke a social and cultural response in her contemporaries. Furthermore, it is a way for her to establish and explore her own spiritual heritage and authority. Annemieke van Drenth suggests that the way Butler's 'holy beliefs reinforced her humanitarianism is apparent from her intense fascination with saints', and that Butler studied their lives in order to deepen her own spirituality.[41] With a more outward perspective, Janet Larson observes that Butler 'was determined to revive' the influence of Saint Catharine as a 'mystic and reformer to put new fire into the campaign, reassert her spiritual leadership of it, and instruct a nation that much needed to know Catherine's [sic] story in 1878'.[42] Larson adds, 'whatever lessons this holy woman's life might teach modern-day England could not come from the visions alone but had to be grounded in the saint's practical experiences and set into a large, complex story as sophisticated as the writer's sense of the actualities of the present'.[43] Saint Catharine's political and social power was as crucial to Butler's hagiographic mission as her sense of divine calling, spiritual conviction and her commitment to working directly with the poor and vulnerable.

Yet Catharine of Siena remains a complicated figure, in part because she has been famed for starving herself to death. In *Holy Anorexia* (1985), Rudolph Bell gives an account of Catharine fasting 'rigorously but not to excess' as a youth, then after her 'conversion to radical holiness', restricting her diet to 'bread, uncooked vegetables, and water'. After her father's death, Bell writes that she 'lost her appetite and could not eat bread', and that by about the age of twenty-five, 'she ate "nothing"'. He also cites Catharine's disciple and early biographer, Raymond: 'Not only did she not need food, but she could not even eat without pain. If she forced herself to eat, her body suffered greatly, she could not digest and she had to vomit'.[44] Caroline Walker Bynum, engaging specifically with Butler's biography of the saint, suggests that Butler did not have a theory of anorexia to use in positioning Catharine's relationship to food, and while Butler understands this aspect of the saint's life as an 'infirmity', she does not dwell on it.[45] Larson holds to Bynum's assessment, suggesting, 'If a month's fasting… hurried on the saint's death at thirty-three, Butler does not dwell on it, nor does she interrogate Catherine's [sic] self-inflicted pain'.[46] However, it is necessary to readdress Catharine of Siena's relationship to food, and Butler's attention to it, in a new way, not imposing late twentieth-century lenses of eating disorders, or even the nineteenth-century phenomena of the fasting girls, in ways that become reductive or try to pathologize away the ethics behind food restraint. This is not to deny that mental illnesses relating to anorexia nervosa or bulimia existed before they had diagnoses, or even physical illnesses such as coeliac disease that can create a great deal of pain when one consumes bread, the staple of the medieval Italian diet. It is also not my aim to suggest that what begins as an ethical choice cannot lead into paths of extremity, such as experienced by Jane Plymley who began at fourteen, along with her family, to restrict her consumption to enable more food to be available to the poor, but 'whose severe dietary abstinence proved fatal'. Even so, it is important to note that her aunt Katherine Plymley does not write of her niece as 'a fading flower of femininity but as an ethical (if misguided) economic agent'.[47] Dalley and Rappoport understand 'Jane's private, bodily actions' not just as 'part of the gentry's wider emphasis on restricted consumption and moral economy', but her starvation becomes associated with her 'thwarted desire for the larger sphere of public economic action available to her father but not to her'.[48] Gleadle positions Jane Plymley in her aunt's eyes as living 'a quiet life of contemplation and study', much like a cloistered nun, whose 'food denial' came from the 'purest, the most charitable, the most conscientious motives'.[49] The understanding of Jane Plymley's ethical choice is crucial here because it acknowledges her agency in a way that narratives of anorexia nervosa neglect, much as the readings of Catharine of Siena in terms of anorexia nervosa largely discount her ethical conviction that drove the extraordinary influence she had on the fourteenth-century religious and national political landscapes.

The anorexic space that Catharine of Siena inhabits is far more complicated than anachronistic narratives of anorexia nervosa or bulimia, both for the historical Saint Catharine and for Butler's biographical purposes. It is within the liminality of Catharine's anorexic space that Butler locates Catharine's very real social and political power. Catharine's personal, spiritual and social agency is found within liminal spaces that defy categorization; and for Butler, inspired by the fourteenth-century saint, such liminality resonates with the work she is trying to achieve amongst prostitutes – women who are marginal, vulnerable and poor, with precarious food security. Catharine's food restraint focalizes a liminal point between spiritual discipline and social action, and for Butler this connection is key. Thus in spite of Catharine's end being potentially read as self-martyrdom, Butler positions her food restraint, at least initially, as an ethical choice in the face of widespread starvation, and a practical, rational choice of social action, as a means to give the excess – or, at least, what she thought was the excess – of her entire family's food to the poor who had nothing.

The way in which Butler deals with Catharine's food restraint as resisting a culture of excess very much reflects the excess of nineteenth-century Britain. In setting the scene of Catharine's world, Butler writes:

> Many of the old-fashioned virtues had disappeared, and revolting vices prevailed, especially in the courts and palaces of princes, both lay and ecclesiastical. Base intrigues were the order of the day, and the only recognized means of earthly success. The aristocracy set an example of every crime, and the grossest debauchery reigned in their palaces and castles… Magistrates were corrupt, and justice sold… This independent spirit manifested itself in constantly renewed struggles to cast off the yoke, first of one tyrant, and then of another; at one time some aggressive noble, at another of a foreign invader… It was that of a worldly, greedy, grasping power, a power which had lost its influence for good over the conscience

of all Christendom, and had thrown itself into the fierce conflict of arms and intrigue with all who disputed its claims to a despotic material sovereignty.[50]

There is much in this description of corruption, injustice and out-of-control independence that would speak to Butler's nineteenth-century readership, and it is within this context that she situates Catharine,

> the wool-dyer's daughter who first dared to address the Pope at Avignon letters full of severe truth, setting forth to him the miseries of his Italian subjects, the evils of his non-residence, and the gross cruelties of his unworthy legates; it was she who prevailed in her endeavour to bring back the Sovereign Pontiff to his country, and to awaken him to a sense of his responsibilities towards his torn and distracted flock.[51]

Butler thus uses the medieval saint to challenge the complacency and abdication of moral responsibility of her own age.

Early in the biography, Butler writes of the 'peculiar blessing' Catharine received from Christ for having sacrificed family and home for the sake of the gospel: 'And what was that peculiar blessing? In her case, at least, it was a greater *power* – power to win, to convert, to suffer, to rule, to command, for the salvation of erring man, and for the glory of God'[52] Importantly for Butler, Catharine's authority is not restricted to the spiritual: she asserts not just Catharine's power as a moral force, or, translating to the nineteenth century, the private moral, domestic space conventionally available to women. Catharine of Siena had very real influence and authority as an ambassador who moved nations. She had power over two popes and has been historically held responsible for the Great Schism in the Catholic Church. It is also significant to note, however, that Butler's reference to the saint's power follows a substantial level of engagement with Catharine's asceticism and a discussion of varying figures who tried to persuade her to give up her physical disciplines.

Crucially, Catharine of Siena resists the cultural expectations placed upon her, and it is within that resistance that she finds her social power. In particular, she made her family and the institution of the Church uncomfortable; and she did this by refusing to fit with their gendered expectations. When her parents tried to arrange her marriage, Catharine found this option unpalatable. At that time, God conveniently gave her a revelation that she should join the Order of the Dominican nuns. However, rather than joining the Order fully, Catharine became a tertiary, which meant that she lived at home with her parents, rather than in the abbey with the other nuns, and was in many ways outside the strictures of the Order. At the same time, because she was a part of the Order, she was outside the bounds of family responsibility. This was one of the first ways that Catharine facilitated a liminal space to have social autonomy. This mode would influence other aspects of her career and self-identification. In terms of her religion, although very much within the Catholic Church, she almost prided herself in depending on her own connection with the Divine rather than any kind of human spiritual authority. This is something that would have resonated with the distinctly ecumenical nineteenth-century Josephine Butler. Butler prides her minister husband with his broad views in taking on a multicultural school in Liverpool:

> Among its eight to nine hundred pupils there were Greeks, Armenians, Jews, Negroes, Americans, French, Germans, and Spaniards, as well as Welsh, Irish, Scotch and English. These represented many different religious persuasions. A man of narrow theological views would scarcely have found the position as head of such a school agreeable.[53]

Butler's receptiveness to different religious ideas, and her resistance to being tied to any kind of religious or political persuasion, reflects Catharine of Siena's position. Butler could see herself, like her historical counterpart, being in a very biblical sense, in the world, but not of it.

Juxtaposed with Catharine's dietary asceticism is her extraordinary physical strength and stamina. Butler writes of Catharine 'put[ting] forth... the strength of an athlete'. Her spiritual preparations 'were not a time of listless contemplation nor of sentimental piety... They were a stern and energetic preparation for the combats of her future life'. Butler immediately follows this statement with Catharine being 'very sparing in her diet' but notes that she 'allowed no outward marks of asceticism to appear in her person... Catharine's health was delicate, yet she possessed an extraordinary nervous energy, and even a muscular strength which astonished those who saw her exert it in the performance of any generous or helpful act'.[54] Catharine's physical strength is not written as divine intervention so much as Catharine's determination to fulfil her social action. While upholding the saint's spiritual convictions, Butler moves away from ideas of holy or miraculous fasting to position food restraint as an active, rational choice: a form of ethical fasting, as much as it is spiritual. She writes of Catharine discerning those among the poor who were the most needy and *choosing* to give secretly to these families. Butler goes on to say that when Catharine's own provision was 'exhausted, she sought her father, and asked him if she might deduct, according to her conscience, the portion of the poor from the ample means which he had realized in his industry'.[55] According to Butler's account, her father

> cheerfully consented, because he saw clearly that his daughter 'was walking in the way of perfection;' he announced to his assembled family the permission he had granted. 'Let no one,' he said, 'prevent my beloved child from bestowing our goods on the poor. I grant her full liberty; indeed, she may, if she likes, dispense all that is in the house'.

Butler continues: 'Catharine made use almost too literally of the generous permission of her father, so much so, that 'all the inmates of the house, her father excepted, complained of her donations, and locked up what they had that she might not distribute it to the poor'".[56]

Just as Butler wrote more polemically in *Woman's Work and Woman's Culture*, this anecdote illustrates questions regarding necessity and excess, and challenges the unwillingness to sacrifice privilege and social power for the sake of intervening on behalf of the vulnerable. In an implicit manner, she speaks to the waste in urban Britain, and the response of Catharine's father is intended to provoke consciences regarding necessity and the compulsion to consume and horde in light of capitalist endeavour. There is an intention to cultivate an understanding of generosity, and similarly an understanding of one's own privilege, that is conveyed by Catharine and her father, perhaps modelling Butler and her own father, as a foil to the fearful hoarding of the rest of their family, representing nineteenth-century British society. Later, Butler includes an account by Catharine's disciple, Raymond, who noted that when they were ministering to the poor, they often did not eat all day until the evening because Catharine was preoccupied with the needy, and that then Catharine would be more concerned about the 'material wants' of her friends than her own, which made them 'forget [their] fatigues'.[57] Butler uses Catharine's relationship with food to challenge self-focus and encourage an outward vision toward the community. Within the narrative, it is Catharine's willingness to care for others before herself that enabled her to achieve the level of public influence that she gained.

Catharine was a politician and a diplomat, and her food restraint becomes as much about a social vision as a theological one. Butler says that Catharine never took on 'false doctrine', and that her 'efforts were directed solely to moral reformation, her attacks being mainly aimed at the vices, worldliness, and ungodliness of the clergy'.[58] Here Catharine's example speaks most soundly to the social mission of Butler herself. Janet Larson compares Butler and Catharine explicitly: 'Both were charismatic leaders and sought to be a "light to the Church" in their time. A scandal to their contemporaries for stepping outside woman's sphere, they raised opposition and drew persecution, addressed angry mobs undaunted, and narrowly escaped "martyrdom".[59] Indeed, Butler drives home the comparison when she writes,

> There are Christians enough assuredly, in our own days, to whom such arguments as Catharine used to the friars might be very suitably addressed; Christians in whose hearts lies a deep, though it may be an unconscious and unconfessed selfishness. Their ears are dull to the daily cry of the needy and the oppressed, they do not hear the earnest call to join with God's advanced guard in the battle against vice and oppression and diabolic cruelty. The sacred seclusion of their homes is so sweet. They love so much their own secure and safe 'retreat'.[60]

Butler does not suggest that people should give up their secure homes – that would just create more chaos through increased poverty and precarity. Rather she calls on people to recognize their own privilege and have some willingness, like Catharine, to sacrifice some of that privilege to aid those without. The emphasis is on disciplined, conscious restraint, not asceticism. Butler suggests an alternative power to the political and economic power of capitalism when she writes, 'We all have the power... to become honest, truthful, courageous, just, patient, self-denying, and kind. We can all learn to oppose persistently and with courage what we know to be evil'.[61]

While Butler does not shy away from Catharine's death, she focalizes the saint's willingness to give of herself: not in a way that reinforces the limitations on woman's sphere, but in a way that enables power and social action. There is a purpose beyond herself for that power, not just the privilege of having power in and of itself. This power, then, also dwells in a liminal space, moderated through its dependence on an active social vision. The kind of liminality that both Catharine of

Siena and Josephine Butler experience enables them to carve out a different way, taking on influences but not being defined by them, and to be able to speak from a singular perspective of being both within and without, empowered by the impulse of social prophecy in action. Concepts of privilege are tied closely with Butler's social justice. In *Otherwise than Being* (1981), Levinas provocatively contends that one is not truly human until one takes the bread out of one's own mouth to give it to another.[62] Humanity is thus predicated on sacrifice: not just giving out of one's excess but giving at pains to oneself. Giving, in Levinas's view, requires the giver to know what it is, in terms of pleasure or enjoyment, that they are giving up. In terms of Butler's theology, this then extends to fasting, not just in terms of giving food, but in being willing to sacrifice one's own privilege and agency.

Britain's gluttonous capitalism

In *Prophets and Prophetesses*, Butler explicitly addresses the culture of greed and gluttony that she sees as the spirit of the age:

> Never did the world and the Church need Seers more than at the present time. Looking at any of the great questions before us now; – the relations of nation to nation, and of the Anglo-Saxon race to the heathen populations of conquered countries; questions of gold-seeking; of industry; of capital and labour; of the influence of wealth, now so great a power in our country and its dependencies; questions of legal enactments; of the action of Governments; and innumerable social and economic problems, we may ask: – How much of the light of Heaven is permitted to fall on those questions? How many or how few are there among us who ask, and seek, and knock, and wait to know *God's thought* on these matters?[63]

As in her other works, she argues not only that the gluttony of consumerism compromises the health and well-being of the vulnerable, but also that it compromises the health of the privileged. In *Woman's Work* she contends that one cannot

> have read the Scriptures, or history, or human life, at all thoughtfully, without being struck with this – that wherever one class or set of human beings has been placed at a disadvantage as compared with another class, has been deprived of whatsoever just privileges or denied a legitimate share of God's endowment of the world, the class so treated is not always the one for whom our gravest fears admit of the most reasonable justification… the class which suffers most eventually, is not the class which is deprived, oppressed, or denied, but that which deprives, oppresses, or denies.[64]

Butler is not trying to suggest that the wealthy should be pitied more; rather within her theology she holds a belief that justice will prevail on earth, and that the disintegration of moral health will have a material effect. However, what is also crucial in this passage is the requirement to have looked at the Scriptures, history or life *thoughtfully*. Within the incessant need to accumulate, the relentless busyness, there is little time for reflection or constructing a measured purpose. In terms that resonate with Rossetti's writing on the sacredness of the Sabbath, Butler writes of the need to pause and think, and that in the busyness of the age, even those who are most well-intentioned often lack this capacity. She observes that '[m]any even of our holiest men and women live too active, too hurried a life, to be able to enter deeply into the thought of God', and because of this lack are unable 'to speak that thought of God, and thence to speak that thought to the thirsty multitudes who are dimly seeking after Him, and in their hearts crying, "who will show us any good?"'[65] In order to have the prophetic voice, the voice of the divine to bring hope to the 'thirsty multitudes', they need to replenish, take time to be thoughtful, and step aside from the compulsion to consume. Times of solitude are necessary to break the anxious cycle of consumption.

In her theology of solitude, Butler refers to the biblical figure of Daniel, an Old Testament prophet and leader known for his fasting practices, ranging from refusing to eat anything other than vegetables, to times of complete abstinence from food. She writes that it is 'in the solitude of the soul, alone with God, that his thoughts are revealed. It is in great humility, in separation from the spirit of the world, in asking to receive *his* spirit, "the Spirit of Truth" which "shall guide us into all truth," that we learn to think his thoughts'.[66] At the same time, though, she acknowledges that it requires courage to be able to separate oneself from the world in this way, to let go of the need to consume:

> It requires much courage to be alone with God; to elect to retire for a time, and even for long times, and to listen to *his* voice only. It requires more courage than is needed to meet human opposition, or to battle with an outward enemy, and is altogether different from worship in the congregation with others around us... For it is then that the keen search-light of his presence reveals the innermost recesses of the soul, so that the creature, who has been bold enough to seek such a solitary interview with the Creator, shall fall on his face, as Daniel did, in self abasement: – 'I, Daniel, fainted and was sick certain days'.[67]

Butler refers to Daniel 8:27, the end of a chapter detailing one of Daniel's apocalyptic visions of a world self-destructing through arrogance and a consuming desire for power. Thus she suggests that this battle referenced in Daniel is the same one facing late-Victorian Britain. As Rebecca Styler notes, 'Butler's language of the period is full of the rhetoric of spiritual warfare, pitting herself against a spiritual enemy which she saw within the structures of society, supported even by much of its liberal progressive element'.[68] Butler acknowledges that courage is necessary 'to listen to *his* voice only' because what one hears will be necessarily troubling as well as transformative.

It was the transformation into action, though, that was most crucial for Butler. In *The Lady of Shunem* (1894), she explicitly uses the biblical account of the Shunemite woman to speak to those who live in privilege, challenging them to rethink the way in which they view and treat those who appear to be of less worth in worldly terms. She encourages her readers to see the likeness of God in all people, regardless of class or creed, by establishing the wisdom and good judgement of this lady of rank. It is less than subtle that Butler points out that the Lady of Shunem appears to be a 'landed proprietress', given the emphasis of Butler's work on women's economic emancipation. However, even more critical is the way the lady uses her wealth and position. Butler notes, 'She had observed the bearing and conduct' of the prophet Elisha. Because she was 'a hospitable woman', she

> earnestly pressed him to stay at her house for refreshment and rest, which he did 'as often as he passed by.' Convinced by further observation of his character – though he was but a poor man, turning in, footsore and hungry, from his pedestrian missions – that he was 'a holy man of God,' she planned, with true womanly tact and kindness, that he should have a room of his own in her house, a permanent abode, to which he could freely come at all times.[69]

Deliberately playing on her readers' consternation at this apparently immoral act of a wanton woman creating a room for a single man in her home, Butler delays mention of the Shunemite's husband. Even so, it is evident that in suggesting to her husband that they make a chamber for the prophet and his servant, she is not asking permission: Butler presents them as equal in their marriage and home. Butler observes,

> In passing, we may notice her character as a wife, and the worthiness of her husband. Their relations to each other seem to have been of the best and most dignified. She appears to have been of an

independent and self-reliant spirit; and he was wise and worthy of her, granting her the initiative and freedom of judgement and action which her strong and dignified character entitled her to exercise. There was no assumption of superiority or show of masculine rule on the one hand, and no servility or weak dependence on the other. They were a couple worthy of admiration and imitation.[70]

Within the story of the Shumenite woman and her husband, Butler implicitly tells her own tale of taking prostitutes and poor women into her own home, radically casting the outcast in the role of the prophet. With such biblical precedent, Butler justifies both her private actions in terms of her embracing these women, and her public role as supported and celebrated by a wise and discerning husband in George Butler. Their actions and convictions are divinely ordained and an expression of dignity, good judgement and hospitality, as well as the recognition of God's spirit in those who they take into their home. It is within that vein that Butler seeks to challenge society to transform their reception and judgements of the poor and vulnerable with rational compassion.

Duty of the heart and body

As much as Butler had written that it was a mistake to cast women who campaigned for emancipation as bitter and miserable, she also wrote of the way in which her young daughter's tragic death had motivated her to find means by which to help others. 'I became possessed with an irresistible desire', she recalls, 'to go forth and find some pain keener than my own, to meet with people more unhappy than myself (for I knew there were thousands of such).'[71] She writes that she had 'no plan for helping others', but was motivated by a 'sole wish ... to plunge into the heart of some human misery, and to say (as I now knew I could) to afflicted people, "I understand: I too have suffered"'.[72] Butler saw in her tragedy a means to empathize with suffering; and, as she noted, 'It was not difficult to find misery in Liverpool'.[73]

Butler writes of the attempts of many, both Roman Catholic and Protestant, to alleviate poverty in Liverpool, but the level of need overwhelmed the city. She describes visiting the workhouse and the hospital for paupers, and the number of women dying of consumption 'little cared for spiritually' on special wards. On the ground floor of the hospital, the damp, bare and unfurnished 'oakum sheds', women came 'voluntarily... driven by hunger, destitution, or vice, begging for a few nights' shelter and a piece of bread, in return for which they picked their allotted portion of oakum'. Butler emphasizes the destitution of these women by adding 'Others were sent there as prisoners'.[74] Butler recounts that she continued to visit these women, teaching them and praying with them, but such actions were not enough:

> We had a dry cellar in our house and a garret or two, and into these we crowded as many as possible of the most friendless girls who were anxious to make a fresh start. This became inconvenient, and so in time my husband and I ventured to take a house near our own, trusting to find funds to furnish and fill it with inmates. This was the 'House of Rest,' which continued for many years, and developed, about the time we left Liverpool, into an incurable hospital, supported by the town. It was there that, a little later, women incurably ill were brought from the hospitals or their wretched homes, their beds in hospital being naturally wanted for others.[75]

Like her father, Butler needed to enact her spiritual convictions through acts of social justice. She understood fasting as sacrificing some of her own privilege in order to provide agency and equality for others. Just as she had responded to 'the cry of woman' she heard when she read Gaskell's *Ruth* in Oxford, which began 'her battle for both legal and moral justice for women and the poor',[76] she needed, like the medieval saints before her, to act as well as to speak. In her mission, as in her theology, Butler believed in the importance of ministering to the bodies of the vulnerable as much as to their souls.

Notes

1. Josephine Butler, *Prophets and Prophetesses: Some Thoughts for the Present Times* (London: Dyer Brothers, 1897), 10.
2. Rossetti's Feast Day is 27 April, during the Easter season. Butler's Feast Day is 30 December, the anniversary of her death.
3. Helen Mathers, 'The Evangelical Spirituality of a Victorian Feminist: Josephine Butler, 1828–1906', *Journal of Ecclesiastical History*, 52.2 (2001): 282–312, 283.
4. Josephine E. Butler, Introduction to *Woman's Work and Woman's Culture: A Series of Essays* (London: Macmillan, 1859), vii–lxiv, lii.
5. Ibid., liii.
6. Ibid., liv.
7. Rebecca Styler, 'Josephine Butler's Serial Auto/Biography: Writing the Changing Self through the Lives of Others', *Life-Writing*, 14.2 (2017): 171–84, 171.
8. See Janet L. Larson's 'Josephine Butler's *Catharine of Siena*: Writing (Auto)Biography as a Feminist Spiritual Practice', *Christianity and Literature*, 48.4 (1999): 445–71 and 'Praying Bodies, Spectacular Martyrs, and the Virile Sisterhood: "Salutary and Useful Confusions" in Josephine Butler's *Catharine of Siena*', *Christianity and Literature*, 49.1 (1999): 3–34.
9. Butler, Introduction to *Woman's Work*, 1.
10. Matt. 6:16-18.
11. Josephine Butler, *An Autobiographical Memoir*, ed. George W. and Lucy A. Johnson (Bristol: J. W. Arrowsmith, 1909), 8. Quotation from Is. 58:6.
12. Helen Mathers, '"'Tis Dishonour Done to *Me*": Self-Representation in the Writings of Josephine Butler', in *Sex, Gender, and Religion: Josephine Butler Revisited*, ed. Jenny Daggers and Diana Neal, 37–53 (New York: Peter Lang, 2006), 40.

13 Jane Jordan, *Josephine Butler* (2001; London: Hambledon Continuum, 2007), 3.
14 Mathers, 'Evangelical Spirituality', 294.
15 Alison Milbank, 'Josephine Butler: Christianity, Feminism and Social Action', in *Disciplines of Faith: Studies in Religion, Politics and Patriarchy*, ed. Jim Obelkevich, Lyndal Roper and Raphael Samuel, 154–64 (London: Routledge, 1987), 155.
16 Ibid., 155–6.
17 Jenny Daggers and Diana Neal, Introduction to *Sex, Gender, and Religion: Josephine Butler Revisited*, 1–19 (New York: Peter Lang, 2006), 14.
18 Butler, *An Autobiographical Memoir*, 5.
19 Ibid., 6–8.
20 Lucretia A. Flammang, '"And Your Sons and Daughters Will Prophesy": The Voice and Vision of Josephine Butler', in *Women's Theology in Nineteenth-Century Britain: Transfiguring the Faith of Their Fathers*, ed. Julie Melnyk, 151–64 (New York and London: Garland Publishing, 1998), 152.
21 Jordan, *Josephine Butler*, 17–18.
22 Ibid., 2.
23 Ibid., 3.
24 Flammang, '"And Your Sons and Daughters Will Prophesy"', 152.
25 Ibid., 153.
26 Kathryn Gleadle, 'Gentry, Gender, and the Moral Economy during the Revolutionary and Napoleonic Wars in Provincial England', in *Economic Women: Essays on Desire and Dispossession in Nineteenth-Century British Culture*, ed. Lana L. Dalley and Jill Rappoport, 25–40 (Columbus: Ohio State University Press, 2013), 34–5.
27 Ibid., 35.
28 Ibid., 32.
29 Ibid., 33–4.
30 Butler, *Woman's Work*, ix.
31 Ibid.
32 Ibid., x.

33 Ibid., x–xi.
34 Ibid., xi.
35 Ibid., xii.
36 Ibid. Emphasis added.
37 Ibid., xvi.
38 Ibid., xv.
39 Ibid., xxv–xxvi.
40 Ibid., xxvi. Emphasis orig.
41 Annemieke van Drenth, 'Holy Beliefs and Caring Power: Josephine Butler's Influence on Abolitionism and the Women's Movement in the Netherlands (1850–1920)', in *Sex, Gender, and Religion: Josephine Butler Revisited*, ed. Jenny Daggers and Diana Neal, 73–95 (New York: Peter Lang, 2006), 77.
42 Larson, 'Josephine Butler's *Catharine of Siena*', 445–6.
43 Ibid., 461.
44 Rudolph M. Bell, *Holy Anorexia* (Chicago and London: University of Chicago Press, 1985), 28.
45 Caroline Walker Bynum, *Holy Feast and Holy Fast: The Religious Significance of Food to Medieval Women* (Berkeley: University of California Press, 1987), 168–9.
46 Larson, 'Praying Bodies', 15.
47 Lana L. Dalley and Jill Rappoport, 'Introducing Economic Women', in *Economic Women: Essays on Desire and Dispossession in Nineteenth-Century British Culture*, 1–21 (Columbus: Ohio State University Press, 2013), 6.
48 Ibid.
49 Gleadle, 'Gentry, Gender and the Moral Economy', 36.
50 Josephine Butler, *Catharine of Siena: A Biography* (3rd ed. 1878; London: Horace Marshall & Son, 1894), 5–7.
51 Ibid., 11–12.
52 Ibid., 43.
53 Butler, *Autobiographical Memoir*, 57.
54 Butler, *Catharine of Siena*, 31–2.
55 Ibid., 68–9.

56 Ibid., 69.
57 Ibid., 89.
58 Ibid., 239.
59 Larson, 'Josephine Butler's *Catharine of Siena*', 446.
60 Butler, *Catharine of Siena*, 269.
61 Ibid., 336–7.
62 Emmanuel Levinas, *Otherwise than Being or Beyond Essence*, trans. Alphonso Lingis (1981; Pittsburgh: Duquesne University Press, 1998), 74.
63 Butler, *Prophets and Prophetesses*, 10–11.
64 Butler, *Woman's Work*, viii–ix.
65 Butler, *Prophets and Prophetesses*, 4.
66 Ibid., 11–12.
67 Ibid., 12.
68 Styler, 'Josephine Butler's Serial Auto/biography', 178.
69 Josephine Butler, *The Lady of Shunem* (London: Horace Marshall & Son, 1894), 9–10.
70 Ibid., 10–11.
71 Butler, *Autobiographical Memoir*, 58.
72 Ibid., 58–9.
73 Ibid., 59.
74 Ibid.
75 Ibid., 61–2.
76 Jordan, *Josephine Butler*, 46.

4

Alice Meynell's fasting and the health of the body

It came natural to her to do without so that other people might have. She did without leisure so that other people might have share of her leisure... The open hand of hospitality! The real spirit of austerity which made her turn away from the comfortable and soft things women far more robust than she seek after! There were moments when one of those who loved her ached to give her the luxuries she would have put away if they had been offered to her.
– Katharine Tynan, 'Mrs. Meynell and Her Poetry', 1913[1]

In *Food, Morals and Meaning* (2000), John Coveney addresses the role of nutrition in defining morality in food consumption. He observes that the science of nutrition 'did not invent a morality about eating, even if it rehearses it. Nutrition merely mapped onto existing concerns about food and pleasure that have been a part of Western culture since antiquity'.[2] He adds, 'food pleasure was considered to be problematic, principally because pleasures derived from food undermined a more rational and reasoned approach to eating'.[3] Coveney's argument is embedded within well-established scholarship on the history of social anxieties related to the enjoyment of food and other types of consumption. What is particularly crucial in his work is the way in which he draws out the role of science in legitimizing such anxieties:

> Nutrition provides a guide for individuals to assess their eating habits in terms of what is 'good'. Indeed, the term 'good food', once reserved for notions of tables laden with tasty dishes of food, now

suggests something entirely different. Today good food requires one to show less concern with the physical pleasure of eating, and more interest in the good health that results from our dietary habits... These comments signal the way in which scientific and technical knowledge forms the basis for the moral judgements we make about ourselves and others. It is this moral imperative which is encoded in nutrition that makes it so compelling, so engaging, so judgemental, and so strangely popular... it would seem that we are fascinated by the moral dimensions of food choice: what we should and should not be eating.[4]

Although Coveney's study engages more thoroughly with the late twentieth century, he is extremely aware of the heritage of scientific development, especially the development of nutrition as a discrete scientific field in the nineteenth century, that impacted moral, ethical and spiritual understandings of consumption. The mid-nineteenth century saw the adoption of calories from physics into physiology and animal chemistry, with the German physician, chemist and physicist Julius Robert von Mayer, one of the founders of thermodynamics, publishing two papers between 1846 and 1848 engaging with energy metabolism and the relation between physical work and gravity, and the energy supplied by food in terms of kilograms and calories.[5] The German school of physiology influenced the British and American developments of nutritional science, 'introduc[ing] proximate analysis and calorimetry to determine the least expensive sources of nutritionally balanced foods', and, more generally, the 'physiological energy value' of different foods, especially proteins.[6] This scientific work developed in an imperialist Britain that had a long heritage of valuing a meat-heavy diet as a symbol of strength and power. Therefore the science of 'good' or 'bad' food in the sense of which foods, as well as how much food, was considered healthy or necessary becomes complicated by the cultural context in which it emerges, at the same time that it lends authority to cultural preconceptions.[7]

As well as the scientific turn toward the calorie in nutrition, mid-nineteenth-century physiology was influenced by the increased understanding of humans as a part of the natural world, and the interconnectedness of that world. The Dutch physician Jacob Moleschott, who also studied in Germany, wrote of 'the sacred sense of necessary dependence' between all of nature.[8] He concludes his preface to *The Chemistry of Food and Diet* (1856), his only work that was translated into English, with the words of the German naturalist and ethnographer Georg Forster:

> Nature can change, transform, dissolve, develop, renew everything, but cannot create or annihilate anything. The quantity of matter existing, remains always the same. But no form remains constant, not even man himself. The matter of which all bodies consist, is in a perpetual flux; the same material is continually appearing under another form.[9]

Although Moleschott himself was an atheist, his language readily resonates with that of incarnational and Eucharistic theology, not just in the way he adopts the term 'sacred' to describe the interdependence of all of nature, including humanity, but also in the way nature becomes one organism – one body, like the Body of Christ. Crucially for theology, Moleschott's concept is centred on the blood: all nourishment turns into blood. It is the circulation of nourishment and decay, veins and arteries, that feeds the body until that body decomposes to nourish the earth once more. It is the blood that enables the perpetual change in matter, and a revisioning of life and death. Blood enables the cycle of nourishment and decay. But life and death are reconstituted in terms of transformation and transition within an absolute, eternal concept of nature – Moleschott's 'Grand Circle'[10] – of which humans form just a part. Yet Moleschott asserts that it is a part bestowed with responsibility, given the level of sentience and reasoning available to humanity. Humans, to varying degrees, have a choice of what to eat, and therefore how to nourish and form the blood; and such choices must be made with a moral consciousness of the place of humanity within the natural world. Moleschott's view extends into a concept of public health that then extends to the health of the entire system, a health found in the circulation of healthy blood, nourished by a healthy diet.

Alice Meynell's relationship to food and fasting illuminates the connections between scientific models that understood the role of blood in circulating and transforming nutrition, the interdependence of society in Christian Socialism, the theological underpinnings of the Eucharist and the Church as the Body of Christ, and poetry's dynamic interconnection of every part. Her Roman Catholic incarnational theology emphasizes the reverence of the Body of Christ, the Blood of Christ, and the interconnectedness of the Body's members, while her Christian Socialism undergirds her belief in working actively to correct social inequalities in a material sense. Socialism understands society as an interdependent body, which adheres to Meynell's theological understanding as well as that of the other women in this study.[11] The morality or immorality of consumption was deeply embedded in Meynell's moral and ethical beliefs, as well as her interest in diets and nutrition from adolescence. Meynell's relationship with food was extremely complex because she had some severe health issues, including that by the age of twenty she had had so many tooth extractions that she needed dentures, and so even the act of eating itself was presumably painful and unpleasant. However, she was also well-known for being frugal in her groceries with the deliberate purpose of giving the money she would have otherwise spent on them to charity. Her lived sense of ethics, social justice and social action was palpable. Turning to ethics creates a tension between potential medical or psychological reasons for fasting, often understood in terms of disorder, with outwardly focused attitudes toward social justice. For Meynell, although fasting was about disciplining her body in spiritual terms, her austerity was not wholly for the sake of her own spiritual and physical health, but also a way to make real room for the poor – to have more money and food in order to provide for them, as promoted in Orthodox, Anglican and Roman Catholic theologies of fasting.

Meynell's fasting and dietary restraint

In spite of Meynell's formidable presence in the late nineteenth-century literary world, scholarship on her life remains sparse. June Badeni's *The Slender Tree* (1981) remains one of the few comprehensive biographies and leans heavily on the 1929 memoir written by Meynell's daughter Viola. In recent years there has been growing interest in this poet, journalist and editor, who was president of the Society of Women Journalists, twice touted for Poet Laureate, and an influential figure in the women's suffrage movement. Through her life and work, and the integrity by which the two were entwined, Alice Meynell had a significant impact on the British social vision. Badeni writes almost hagiographically of Meynell:

> As in her work, so in her life. There, too, was abstention, rejection, discipline; abstention from that which was unworthy, rejection of that which was cheap, discipline of the wild emotions, the wayward passions, the hasty, the uncontrolled. She saw, when she was scarcely grown up, the shape that she wished her spiritual life to take, and she perceived that without the bonds of a moral law she could never attain it, never be wholly free of the domination of heart and passions.[12]

Fasting was central to Meynell's spiritual discipline, but her understanding of spiritual practice was deeply integrated with her understanding of the natural world, physical health and strength, and a sense of justice mixed with frugality in her convictions on consumption. She participated in different kinds of fasting, from full abstention, fasting according to the liturgical calendar, to vegetarianism. But she also knew what it meant to struggle financially, which sometimes influenced her own consumption while also giving her empathy for the impoverished in both Britain and abroad.

Meynell's childhood was somewhat nomadic, with her parents moving her and her sister, Elizabeth, between Britain and the Continent, rarely staying in one place for long. When Meynell was seventeen, the family settled in Bonchurch on the Isle of Wight for almost two years, but during this period the family suffered some financial difficulties which led them to change their standard and means of living. Viola Meynell cites her mother's diary from that time:

> We have had a great disappointment to-day in the matter of money affairs – some mistake of the lawyers. So instead of having a jolly fortnight in London and then going to Germany, we must retire into some cheap country place. To-day I have shed more tears I think than I have before in all my life. I went round the garden and into every nook, and watered the grass with my tears. Tears to me are most poignant agony, a mark of the utmost extremity of pain. They do not come in torrents, but by twos and threes, and each one seems to break my heart. Now it seems to me that I must live on memories, that the sun of my life set behind the down which hid Bonchurch from my aching eyes. The sorrow in my soul is beyond words, beyond all expression, beyond the comprehension of happy spirits. That my life will ever be happy again, I cannot believe.[13]

This passage from the young Meynell's diary at this moment of sudden transition is telling of her response to much of life's experiences. Apart from the aesthetic description of her despair, the way in which she describes her tears as 'not com[ing] in torrents, but by twos and threes' reveals how early on she maintained a sense of restraint in her responses to life. That restraint has been noted in criticism of her poetry and journalism, but, as Badeni notes, was an extension of her lived experience. It also opened her eyes to the struggles of others, for example, the writer Francis Thompson whom Meynell and her husband took under their wing. In a letter to Katharine Tynan from June in 1888, Meynell wrote, 'The author has been selling matches in the Strand for two years. We thought we might rescue him by publishing his things, but alas! we seem to have frightened him away even from the Strand, for he has disappeared. Even hunger does not press him to come for money, though I fear he is famishing'.[14] Meynell did manage a lifelong friendship with Thompson, however, and was instrumental in both saving him from poverty and promoting his literary career.

The Meynells were known for their generosity and concern for others, yet they were also well-known for their personal austerity. Viola Meynell recalls:

> My mother had a particularly gracious way of welcoming a guest. It was so inconceivable to her that everything should not be suitable for the entertainment of anyone who came that she offered even very plain hospitality with the slight ceremony that went with the assumption that it was good... Richard Whiteling, whose long friendship dated from these days, in his reminiscences describes the fare at the Sunday evening suppers as being no more plentiful than 'just to serve, like the banquets in the Iliad, to put away from you the desire of eating and drinking as a hindrance to the flow of soul.' Another writer of reminiscence has related how, after a great deal of talk in the drawing-room, he was invited into the quiet of the library by his host who promised him a treat which his thirst made him interpret in a happy manner. Reaching the library he found his refreshment to consist of having Francis Thompson's early poems read aloud to him. Francis Thompson himself habitually carried up from the table with him a piece of dry bread which he lodged on the library or drawing-room mantelpiece, and which said that his hunger was not appeased.[15]

Explanations for this seeming lack of hospitality could be attributed to severe religious austerity, financial difficulties, or even to a preoccupation toward literature to the neglect of physical appetite, which suggests a kind of Kafkaesque idea of the hunger artist, eschewing all earthly or bodily sustenance, 'diet[ing] in all directions' in order to create, which Leslie Heywood connects to anorexia nervosa.[16] However, it is also possible that the Meynells' attitude toward the consumption of food also came from what they believed to be healthful dietary practice, influenced a great deal by Thomas Low Nichols, an American physician and nutritionist who Alice Meynell and her sister first encountered at a spa on the Continent when the girls were adolescents. Like Meynell, Nichols converted to Roman Catholicism, and therefore held to Catholic ideas of nature, the connection of the natural world, and also ideas of restraint in consumption. To connect to the literary preoccupation of the Meynells, Nichols wrote: 'Wordsworth was a vegetarian. Sir Walter Scott wrote his stories on an empty stomach. The intellect is never no clear and vigorous as after a long fast'.[17] However, Nichols's influence on Alice Meynell is rooted, not so much in the desire for a clear mind brought on by fasting, but for physical health and strength, as well as frugality.

Badeni writes of Elizabeth, in 1868, being concerned that her sister was living on a vegetarian diet, and surmises,

> The diet may have been recommended by the doctor, but it seems more likely that Alice had been persuaded to take to it by Mr and Mrs Nichols, the strange and rather bogus pair under whose guidance the two girls had lived on grapes and sour milk at the watering-place on the Rhine some years before, and who had now turned up at Malvern.[18]

Yet Badeni's claim here follows a paragraph in which she writes specifically of the difficulties the family had been having with paying a butcher's bill, and so it would seem that if the Nicholses were influencing Alice Meynell at this point, it would be in regard to how to live healthily and cheaply without meat, given that they were struggling to afford it. In 1871, Nichols published a pamphlet entitled *How to Live on Sixpence a Day*, published in America the following year with the title change to a dime and a half a day, which encourages vegetarianism as not only the most healthy of diets for humans, but a means by which to live more cheaply without sacrificing necessary nutrition. He writes:

> I wish to show that a simple and cheap diet is not only sufficient for the perfect nourishment of the body, but conducive to strength of mind and serenity of soul, and that living on a dime and a-half a-day may be made even more delightful to the senses than indulgence in costly and pernicious luxuries, and that a pure and simple diet may be as appetizing and delicious as it is healthful and invigorating.[19]

He does promote the 'grape-cure' that Badeni derides; however it is a short-term measure which he uses as a foil to the 'luxuries and indulgences which are sure to bring disease' that he identifies in the regular, unmoderated diet.[20] Importantly, he argues that 'Every ounce of food eaten beyond our needs is a real injury', and goes on to explain,

> The truth is that most people eat too much. Half their strength goes to dispose of surplus food. A well-to-do Englishman eats five meals a-day, when two would be better for him. He consumes two or three pounds of food, and perhaps a larger quantity of drink, when he would be better nourished and sustained by half, or one-third the quantity.[21]

Later, in *The Diet Cure* (1881), Nichols wrote that 'The utmost that any one should take is three meals a-day, and the last should be the lightest and easiest to digest, and should be eaten at least six hours before retiring to rest. Then there is some chance for the stomach to recover its tone in the hours of sleep, and of a good appetite for breakfast'.[22] In terms resonant with theological ideas of the sabbath and fasting, as well as earlier medical texts like Robert Bentley Todd's *Remarks on Fasting* (1848), Nichols adds: 'Remember that for every disease of every organ of the body, the first condition is rest – rest for stomach, rest for brain. Broken bones, and cut or torn muscles, must have rest, or there can be no cure. For the vital organs there must be, at least, diminished labour – intervals of rest – all the repose that is consistent with the necessary operations of life', and further, 'The more rest we can give to the stomach, the more chance for it its own recuperation, and that of all the organs which it supplies with nourishment'.[23]

Meynell's early theological convictions, as well as her health issues, would have resonated with Nichols's nutritional theories. There are accounts in her own diaries as well as her letters and her mother's diary that indicate the frustration she felt with her teeth from a young age, as well as the trauma of seeing the dentist and having her teeth pulled.[24] She also experienced pulmonary illness from childhood, which affected her long-term health, and therefore lends evidence to the idea that her interest and participation in various diets was related to a desire to develop her physical strength rather than preoccupations with austerity for its own sake. However, there were also moments when there was a battle between her capacity to assert her agency, usually articulated through her spirituality and religious practice, against her perceived physical weakness. In her diary of Wednesday, 9 March 1870 she records, 'Up early and to Mass at the Gesù e Maria. Home to breakfast, (I am not allowed to fast) cut my finger to the bone and rushed off to Miss Lloyds who had offered to take me to see the Hospital of S. Michele with the Franchis'.[25] Wednesdays and Fridays are fast days according to the liturgical calendar, and it would appear initially that Meynell was being prevented – perhaps by family, perhaps by her doctor – from fasting, presumably because she has been too extreme in the practice. However, her journal also notes that two days later she is due to be leeched, and it was common practice to not have patients fast before a leeching so as not to diminish their health further.[26] It would seem that her frustration is directed at the weakness of her body in that her ill health, which required her to be leeched, was preventing her from participating in a spiritual practice that she valued. It is also ironic that she cut her finger so badly, perhaps reducing the need for the leeching in the first place, an addition to her self-narrative that reasserts her agency over her own health in a somewhat macabre manner.

Poetry as theology of the body

Meynell understands the tension undergirding her spiritual journey through poetry:

> In quite early childhood I lived upon Wordsworth. I don't know that I particularly enjoyed him, but he was put into my hands, and to me Wordsworth's poetry was the normal poetry *par excellence*. When I was about twelve I fell in love with Tennyson, and cared for nothing else until, at fifteen, I discovered first Keats and then Shelley. With Keats I celebrated a kind of wedding. The influence of Shelley upon me belongs rather to my spiritual than my mental history. I thought the whole world was changed for me thenceforth. It was by no sudden counter-revolution, but slowly and gradually that I returned to the hard old common path of submission and self-discipline which soon brought me to the gates of the Catholic Church.[27]

The legacy of the Oxford Movement and its emphasis on poetry enables Meynell to understand poetry as theology, and therefore as a way to understand how to live. Before converting to Roman Catholicism, Meynell participated in the High Anglicanism that developed out of the revival the Oxford Movement had instigated.

In 'The Tow Path' (1910) Meynell writes, 'To walk unbound is to walk in prose, without the friction of the wings of metre, without the sweet and encouraging tug upon the spirit and the line'.[28] Poetry, like theology, provides a restraint that, while binding, enables one to not feel alone: it is embracing and encouraging, and propels one forward in security. Similarly, in perhaps her most famous essay, 'The Rhythm of Life' (1889), she begins, 'If life is not always poetical, it is at least metrical. Periodicity rules over the mental experience of man, according to the path of the orbit of his thoughts'.[29] It is through this periodicity, whether through poetry or liturgy, that one is able to regulate life and learn that 'presence does not exist without absence', and further that because of life's recurrences, 'Delight can be compelled beforehand, called, and constrained to our service'.[30] Unlike the eighteen-year-old Alice Meynell despairing over her family's financial loss, believing she will never be happy again, the more mature Meynell understands the ebbs and flows of life and has a sense of power and agency beyond those tides. As Amanda Farage observes, this understanding goes beyond the regulation of the individual to the understanding not just of humanity as a whole but, in Catholic terms, to that of the entire natural world: 'as poetry is regulated by meter, pauses, and cadences, the natural world and human experience must follow habitual patterns of activity and rest and creation and stagnation... Meynell declares that everything in life is under the command of life's natural rhythm'.[31] Farage argues that Meynell steps away from the aestheticism of her colleagues such as Walter Pater and Oscar Wilde and 'instead affirms the impossibility of living a "balanced" life at all times (balanced in this instance referring to a static state of being – either living spartanly or in excess), instead acknowledging that we live through a continuous loop of ups and downs', but in this oscillation there is necessary order: 'Rhythm itself... is comprised of a fixed, constant revolution between states, sounds, or beats'.[32]

The liturgical calendar similarly recognizes and honours this periodicity through the regularity of feasts and fasts, with weekly and seasonal shifts, and the interconnectedness of nutritional science, theology and society becomes more palpable through the oscillating rhythms of poetry. As Nichols, Robert Bentley Todd, Jacob Moleschott and other physicians had argued, whether or not of a theological turn themselves, the stomach, as central to the well-being of the entire body, also needs to be regulated through the rhythms of labour and rest or, eating and fasting, to prevent being given to the excess that brings disease to the individual and, by extension, to all of society. Meynell closely associates the poet with medieval saints, writing:

> The souls of certain saints, being singularly simple and single, have been in the most complete subjection to the law of periodicity. Ecstasy and desolation visited them by seasons. They endured, during spaces of vacant time, the interior loss of all for which they had sacrificed the world. They rejoiced in the uncovenanted beatitude of sweetness alighting in their hearts. Like them are the poets whom, three times or ten times in the course of a long life, the Muse has approached touched, and forsaken... Few poets have fully recognized the metrical absence of their muse. For full recognition is expressed in one only way – silence.[33]

Silence, desolation, absence and forsakenness all speak to the fast. While a spiritual practice, it has a specific purpose in creating an ironic connection, not just to the divine, but to the natural world, which encompasses all of humanity – in its rightful place of discipline, a tension between subjection and responsibility. The rites and rituals of the liturgy, like the bonds of poetry, reinforce this position, with that of the Eucharist in particular creating the bond through blood – what Moleschott argues all nutrition turns to, and what all are ultimately dependent on and connected through.

In 'The Unknown God' (1913),[34] Meynell uses the carriers of the Eucharist – 'the Paten and the Cup'[35] as the carriers of this understanding of connection and flow from one being to another. All are connected, all are one, the Body of Christ that must need be kept in wellness through the rhythms of periodicity, through the restraint of body and soul:

> One of the crowd went up,
> And knelt before the Paten and the Cup,
> Received the Lord, returned in peace, and prayed
> Close to my side; then in my heart I said:
>
> 'O Christ, in this man's life –
> This stranger who is Thine – in all his strife,
> All his felicity, his good and ill,
> In the assaulted stronghold of his will,
>
> 'I do confess Thee here,
> Alive within this life; I know Thee near
> Within this lonely conscience, closed away
> Within this brother's solitary day.
>
> 'Christ in his unknown heart,
> His intellect unknown – this love, this art,
> This battle and this peace, this destiny
> That I shall never know, look upon me!
>
> 'Christ in his numbered breath,
> Christ in his beating heart and in his death,
> Christ in his mystery! From that secret place
> And from that separate dwelling, give me grace'.

The mystery of the divine lies in the connection between the poetic speaker and the communicant: although unknown to each other, the communicant's participation in the Eucharist connects the speaker to the divine through the recognition of Christ in the stranger. It is immaterial that they are unknown to each other, for that acknowledgement reflects the knowledge that God, too, is unknown. The reverence of this sacred moment of distance, absence and the unknown encapsulates the sacredness of the fast, which ironically brings recognition of both solitude and community. In consuming the same small portion of bread and wine, they are brought together in abstemious consumption and, like the transubstantiated bread and wine they ingest, are mutually transformed in that moment into the Body and Blood of Christ. The recognition of the imagined, unknown periodicity of this man and of Christ's passion in him, brings solace to the speaker through shared solitude and human limitations: the 'secret place' and 'separate dwelling' of Christ in the communicant gives the speaker grace. Conversely, as a communicant herself, Meynell recognizes her capacity to give such grace to others through Christ in her, both in spite of and because of the fragility of human life.

Meynell was acutely aware of her body's limitations, as well as the material and social limitations placed on her, alongside her spiritual desires. At the same time, she was able to use these experiences to understand the position of others, recognizing through her theological understanding of the Body of Christ that the suffering of a part affects the whole. In her ode 'To the Body' (1906),[36] the intense sensory experience she engages with reflects the awareness of the body that her restraint has focalized – when the tastes, smells and textures of food are made more acute because of that absence. It is in this understanding that the appreciation of the lack that others experience comes into play. It is also in the discipline of the body that one recognizes the authority one has over one's body, and therefore a sense of empowerment that one can choose for that body to act – essentially to alleviate injustice. The materiality of the body also invokes the Eucharist – the complex understandings of the doctrines regarding the Body and Blood of Christ, as well as the community as the metaphorical Body of Christ. It is the Body of Christ that is meant to intervene in the face of social injustice. 'To the Body' presents the authority and responsibility of the disciplined body in a fragmented, chaotic community:

>   Thou inmost, ultimate
> Council of judgement, palace of decrees,
> Where the high senses hold their spiritual state,
>   Sued by earth's embassies,
> And sign, approve, accept, conceive, create;
>
>   Create – thy senses close
> With the world's pleas. The random odours reach
> Their sweetness in the place of thy repose,
>   Upon thy tongue the peach,
> And in thy nostrils breathes the breathing rose.
>
>   To thee, secluded one,
> The dark vibrations of the sightless skies,
> The lovely inexplicit colours run;
>   The light gropes for those eyes.
> O thou august! thou dost command the sun.
>
>   Music, all dumb, hath trod
> Into thine ear her one effectual way;
> And fires and cold approach to gain thy nod,
>   Where thou call'st up the day,
> Where thou awaitest the appeal of God.

The impulse to discipline the body is written through an ethical stance of recognizing the grotesque nature of excess in a world in which there is significant deprivation. The individual's body – not their mind or their heart – is the arena in which social impulses are formed. The body is the 'ultimate | Council of judgement, palace of decrees', and the 'high senses' hold spiritual state within this palace, not the spirit or soul, nor the Holy Spirit. Meynell asserts that it is through the senses individuals perceive the world, including the perception of want. 'Sued by earth's embassies' gives an impression of the world presenting the individual with its concerns in legal terms, as though it has a legal right to petition the individual for action. The senses determine the extent to which one sees the poverty, hears the cries of the suffering, and the willingness to act: to 'sign, approve, accept, conceive, create'.

It is important that 'create' is repeated across the first two stanzas, and the capacity to act very quickly becomes a command to intervene. The entire poem turns on 'thy senses close | With the world's pleas', an interrogation of the willingness with which individuals close their eyes and ears to the plight of others. The double entendre of 'close' meaning near and 'close' meaning to shut provides an ironic space in which Meynell suggests that even when people are so near suffering, they refuse to see it. It stands to reason, then, that she follows this observation with a sensory invasion: 'The random odours reach | Their sweetness in the place of thy repose, | Upon thy tongue the peach, | And in thy nostrils breathes the breathing rose'. There is an irony in these aesthetically pleasing smells, tastes and touches. In the belief of the sensory spontaneity and randomness, Meynell challenges the underlying compulsion to ignore other odours – death, decay and dank do not seem to impose themselves on the body in the same way that the peaches and roses do. They are not so random after all. Although written in aesthetic terms, the sensorily selective body is criticized in the following stanza. The image of the light *groping* for the eyes of the one who refuses to see, who desires to seclude themselves from the trials of the world, of the dark vibrations creating a noise to counteract the sightless skies, speaks to a world that refuses to be ignored. The final line of that stanza, 'O thou august! thou dost command the sun', provides a crucial address to the distinguished position of the body. In a world in which it is easy to feel paralysed by the overwhelming nature of poverty and social trauma, the individual, through the representation of the body, is reminded that it can be 'in command of the sun'. Meynell gives agency to the body with purpose and responsibility: one *can* do something, and the belief that one is powerless is a myth that sustains selfishness, greed, excess and complacency.

The final stanza reveals the persistence of sound – the music invading the ears that cannot be closed easily, the same pathway of the 'dark vibrations' of the previous stanza. Music is paradoxical here – again an aesthetic turn, but the sense of it treading into the ears conjures images of marching, as though protest is the only effective way to gain attention *and* the legal approval referenced in the first verse. Importantly, the body, called upon to show mercy, is placed in subjection to God, which is the position that fasting is meant to evoke. The final two lines are deliberately hierarchical, with the reference to the body's power to '[call] up the day', a further reference to the body's power to 'command the sun', therefore its power, juxtaposed with the greater authority of God. This final line reminds the individual that in their power to choose to see, to hear, to feel, to act, they will ultimately be answerable to God for their actions and inaction. As much as the body is an individual body that makes choices in responding to hunger, poverty and social injustice, the body to which Meynell speaks is also the Body of Christ, so a challenge to the Christian Church to do its duty in serving the community – feeding the hungry, clothing the naked – and also to the social body, so the broader British society, including its institutions of power and authority, the ones who have power to legislate for social change. In Meynell's vision, experiencing illness should create empathy for the ill; fasting, empathy for the starving. The paradox of having the authority to command the sun, but simultaneously waiting the appeal of God, moderates the individual body's hubris. The fasting body is alert to its privilege and, as a result, deliberately attempts to moderate its claims. The object of the fast in this sense is to discipline the body – unruly in excesses that lead to illness – without losing control of the fast itself.

Defence of the Catholic social mission

Although Meynell converted to Roman Catholicism at the age of twenty, from a very young age she was influenced by the

Anglo-Catholicism that emerged from the Oxford Movement. Viola Meynell notes that her mother's conversion was influenced by John Henry Newman's conversion to Rome, but also that it was a conscious, rational decision rather than an emotional or mystical one:

> Catholicism did not take her any far flights into the mystical world she always felt herself unable to explore. Already ardently a Christian, in Catholicism she saw the logical administration of the Christian moral law; and as that she adopted it with a deliberate rational choice, and with what earthly judgement she possessed, more than as a key to the unseen.[37]

For Alice Meynell, religious practice and conviction were meant to be pragmatic, having a material effect on the world that promoted the precepts she held as a Christian Socialist. In *The Poor Sisters of Nazareth* (1889), she promotes fasting and food restraint as an alternative, ethical mode of religious practice that de-emphasizes fasting as a means toward personal spiritual growth. As Jill Rappoport notes in *Giving Women* (2012), the Anglican sisterhoods in England deliberately sought to separate themselves from the Roman Catholic sisterhoods by emphasizing their work among the poor and needy in the community over cloistered devotional practice.[38] It is significant, then, that in her opening statement regarding this Roman Catholic sisterhood, Meynell states that 'Nazareth House, with all the sanctity, shows nothing of the mystery, of the cloister. Reticence there must be, reserve, and silence as to the spiritual experience of these consecrated Sisters, but it is never made apparent'.[39] Later she writes that 'the duties of devotion are always postponed, if necessary, to the duties of charity'.[40] Therefore she emphasizes the social work in which the sisters are engaged, and when she does refer to their spiritual practices, while not minimizing, she seeks to normalize them. This was crucial for Meynell as a Roman Catholic when anti-Catholicism persisted in Britain.

A significant part of the normalizing process is the way Meynell presents the nuns' fasting and food restraint. As nuns they have taken vows of poverty, but Meynell distances this vow from a spiritual motivation to something pragmatic, ethical and socially focused. The first key reference to their austerity is made in relation to a new wing that had been built at Nazareth House. Meynell notes that the wing was necessary so that the nuns could house more homeless people, but also that they needed to rely solely on the alms they received to pay for it. Significantly, she says that the nuns went without themselves in saving the money so none of their dependents would have diminished portions. To avoid going into debt, they 'den[ied] themselves everything except their charities'.[41] This attitude flows into their general approach to food restraint. Meynell describes their austere breakfast of bread and butter, and comments, 'At all their meals they fare like their poor, their food being principally the broken food of alms; and so severe is their abstinence from luxuries, that if game is set to them as a present they touch none of it themselves'.[42]

Meynell uses the ethical example of the Sisters of Nazareth to confront the political state of the nation regarding its consumerism as well as the prominence of political economy in social narratives that justified not giving to the poor. She speaks of the Quest, that is, essentially, begging for food from the surrounding community to give to the poor. The language she uses evokes biblical and medieval allusions, to Christ feeding the five thousand, to the Eucharist, and to the Arthurian quest for the Holy Grail – the cup used in the Last Supper. Meynell writes:

> And what the Quest implies of detailed and minute labour can be but vaguely imagined by those who have not had to pick over and classify and work at the baskets of fragments that remain from the daily breaking of bread in the great consumption of London at its dinner. Everything here is made of scraps, and yet nothing is made of refuse.[43]

The mixed metaphors suggest that beyond feeding the five thousand, what the nuns have access to is the baskets of fragments left over after Christ fed the five thousand – derivative of derivative. More important, though, is Meynell's subtle critique of London, in that the leftovers may be scraps, but they are not rubbish: Londoners are serving themselves an excess and potentially throwing out very good food. She does not overtly state that this waste is obscene but implies it while focusing on the capacity of the nuns to make do.

Meynell's critique of London's excess in the face of want is more overt when she concludes with her description of the sisters' soup kitchen. Almost 2,000 people each day, on top of the dependants who live at Nazareth House, are fed at its gates. Indeed, Meynell notes that often those who live at the House voluntarily give up their share to help in feeding these 'outsiders', many of whom take long journeys across London to find sustenance.[44] Meynell emphasizes that the food provided is excellent, and that no obstacle is put in the way of anyone receiving it. She directly confronts the socio-economic narrative that would suggest that the nuns (and charities in general) are doing more harm than good because they remove the incentive for these figures to find a way to help themselves. She writes:

> It is impossible, looking at these men, silent and uncommunicative and unobservant in their misery, tired with the long tramp that must be heavy payment for a meal, to question the rightness of the Sisters' work of relief. Whatever a riper justice than that of our own time may decide as to the general debt owed by the nation to its poor, the payment of this little matter of interest cannot compromise the larger question. It is the immediate and fugitive succour of want so urgent that no reply is possible except that of the gift in an outstretched hand.[45]

In Meynell's vision, represented in the work of the Sisters of Nazareth, the ethics of food restraint are tied incontrovertibly to the feeding the hungry. As much as she herself maintained austerity in consumption in order to give to the poor, her representation of the nuns elevates the material value of fasting. The nuns are physically strong and outwardly focused despite their fasted lives. Food restraint is not just a spiritual practice, but a means to consume only what is necessary. Meynell adheres to the moderation first learned through Anglicanism, enabling her to narrate a kind of fasting that is both ethical and spiritual, focused outward and upward, while practically benefitting the poor.

Notes

1. Katharine Tynan, 'Mrs. Meynell and Her Poetry', *Catholic World*, 97 (1913): 668–76, 674.
2. John Coveney, *Food, Morals and Meaning: The Pleasure and Anxiety of Eating* (London and New York: Routledge, 2000), viii.
3. Ibid., xii.
4. Ibid., viii.
5. See James L. Hargrove, 'History of the Calorie in Nutrition', *The Journal of Nutrition*, 136.12 (2006): 2957–61.
6. Ibid., 2959–60.
7. Chris Otter's *Diet for a Large Planet* (Chicago: Chicago University Press, 2020) provides an excellent study of the complexities of food ethics in imperial Britain.
8. Jacob Moleschott, *The Chemistry of Food and Diet: With a Chapter on Food Adulterations. Including Constituents of the Human Body, Digestive and Secretive Organs, and the Physiological Principles of Diet*, trans. Edward Bronner and John Scoffern (London: Houlston and Stoneman, 1856), iv.
9. Ibid.
10. Ibid., 19.
11. Elizabeth Ludlow argues that Gaskell reflects on how the 'true Christian' could be 'mistaken for a "socialist and communist"

because of their shared commitment to social justice'. 'Working-Class Methodism', 26.

12 June Badeni, *The Slender Tree: A Life of Alice Meynell* (Padstow, Cornwall: Tabb House, 1981), xi.

13 Viola Meynell, *Alice Meynell: A Memoir* (London: Jonathan Cape, 1929), 36–7.

14 Damian Atkinson, ed., *The Selected Letters of Alice Meynell, Poet and Essayist* (Cambridge: Cambridge Scholars Publishing, 2013), 33.

15 Meynell, *Alice Meynell*, 142.

16 Leslie Heywood, *Dedication to Hunger: The Anorexic Aesthetic in Modern Culture* (Berkeley: University of California Press, 1996), 71.

17 Thomas Low Nichols, *How to Live on a Dime and a-half a-day* (New York: J.S. Redfield, 1872), 26.

18 Badeni, *The Slender Tree*, 39.

19 Nichols, *How to Live*, 6.

20 Ibid., 20.

21 Ibid., 24, 30.

22 Thomas Low Nichols, *The Diet Cure: An Essay on the Relations of Food and Drink, Health, Disease and Cure* (New York: M.L. Holbrook and Co., 1881), 17.

23 Ibid., 18–19

24 See Atkinson, *Selected Letters*, 16 and Meynell, *Alice Meynell*, pp. 18–19.

25 Badeni, *The Slender Tree*, 45.

26 Ibid., 46.

27 Qtd in Meynell, *Alice Meynell*, 42.

28 Alice Meynell, 'The Tow Path', in *Ceres' Runaway & Other Essays* (New York: John Lane, 1910), 89–93, 91.

29 Alice Meynell, 'The Rhythm of Life', in *The Rhythm of Life & Other Essays* (London and New York: John Lane, 1905), 1–6, 1.

30 Ibid., 2–3.

31 Amanda Farage, 'Rhythm of Life, The', in *The Palgrave Encyclopedia of Victorian Women's Writing*, ed. Lesa Scholl and Emily Morris (Palgrave Macmillan, 2021), https://doi.org/10.1007/978-3-030-02721-6_349-1.

32 Ibid.
33 Meynell, 'The Rhythm of Life', 4.
34 In Alice Meynell, *Poems* (London: Burns & Oates, 1913), 99–100.
35 The paten was the sacramental plate used to carry the Eucharistic bread.
36 First published in the *Dublin Review* (1906) and reprinted in *New Catholic World* (1913). In Alice Meynell, *Poems*, 111.
37 Meynell, *Alice Meynell*, 42–3.
38 Jill Rappoport, *Giving Women: Alliance and Exchange in Victorian Culture* (Oxford: Oxford University Press, 2012), 93.
39 Alice Meynell, *The Poor Sisters of Nazareth: An Illustrated Record of Life at Nazareth House, Hammersmith* (1889; New Delhi: Isha Books, 2013), 7.
40 Ibid., 32.
41 Ibid., 10.
42 Ibid., 30–2.
43 Ibid., 16–17.
44 Ibid., 42.
45 Ibid., 44–5.

Conclusion: One body

> *It requires neither a close acquaintance with theology, nor a deep knowledge of medicine, to perceive analogies between religion and health. Both are alike the gift of God. Both are placed in man's hands to be mocked, trifled with, and cast away, or cultivated, treasured, and preserved with ever-increasing joy and satisfaction. They are, perhaps, the two most important things in the world.*
> – Norman Porritt, *Religion and Health*, 1905[1]

The way in which nineteenth-century British medicine, religion and literature entwine in fasting and food restraint, not just as a spiritual discipline, but as an ethical one, and the connection of individual physical health to the health of the community, both come from the slippages between ideas of the individual body, the social body and the Body of Christ. As much as a lot of current research suggests a separation between science and religion, and the nineteenth century in particular as a time when science was being professionalized while religion was moved to the margins, in fact theology and medicine operated dialogically in the nineteenth century, informing and developing each other. Elizabeth Gaskell, Christina Rossetti, Josephine Butler and Alice Meynell were significant because of their public impact. They were incredibly popular writers; however, they also deserve recognition for the theological and social visions they developed through their literary and public engagement. As such, their voices contributed to understandings of health and well-being in nineteenth-century Britain, in terms of both physical health and moral and spiritual wellness.

In the wake of industrialization and developments around chemistry and physiology, medical scientists and some theologians referred to the human body as a machine, and even as a laboratory. But the nineteenth century was also when the idea of a social body became entrenched, wrapped up in ideas of public health as much as the community of the Church, but also in response to the mechanizing metaphors of the social machine – a body, as Catherine Gallagher notes, responds sensorily and has vitality; it is sentient; and it has the capacity either to grow or to die.[2] The health of the nation's body then becomes a symbol for its moral or spiritual health. Pamela Gilbert complicates this idea by asking 'where does the individual body end and the social body begin?... in what consists the boundary between private and public?'[3]

In *The Agency of Eating* (2017), Emma-Jayne Abbots uses the embodied experience of eating to examine the socio-cultural impacts of food consumption and to critique the 'intersections between matter and meaning' that break down the understanding of what the body 'is', 'socially and discursively', in a way that resonates with the indivisibility of the individual and social body.[4] While the embodied experience of eating is mediated by the socio-cultural impacts, this experience simultaneously impacts the definition of the social body. Peter Jackson has also argued that food anxieties cannot be 'understood at a purely individual level' because to do so 'is to neglect the irreducibly social dimensions' of consumer culture.[5] He goes on to suggest that much of the human appetite is a 'vehicle for... psycho-social meaning' and is 'subject to the disciplines of social convention', and therefore that the study of appetite is fundamental to 'distinguishing... the material from the symbolic, self from Other'.[6] Yet what such attention shows is the ultimate indistinguishability between the self and Other and, within the theologies of the women addressed in this study, it is the divine equality of self and Other, and the equal sacredness of the material and the symbolic, that undergird their sense of ethics and social justice. There is no meaningful boundary between private and public, self and Other: all is one divinely infused Body of Nature.

Public health and the Body of Christ

In Robert Lee's *What Christianity Teaches Respecting the Body* (1857), almost a decade after the first Public Health Act was passed in Britain in 1848, there is a decided theological turn toward social responsibility and individual nutrition. This sermon has almost constant slippages between the individual and the social body, while also emphasizing how entwined body and soul are: neither can be classed separately as 'man', rather both are necessary to have that classification.[7] It is in this close interdependence that Lee argues for the need to look after our bodies, and suggests that things to be avoided in this endeavour include bad or insufficient food, as well as intemperance.[8] He then links these aspects directly to public health in a way that previous medical doctors and theologians could not. Therefore, Lee's connection of individual health to the social body, speaking of preventable diseases, the 'constitution of society' and the 'laws of health' reveals the development of a vocabulary around public health and nutrition that became available through the nineteenth century.[9]

In Lee's social vision there is an understanding of the body and its relationship to the social body in spiritual as well as economic terms, written through material health concerns like cholera epidemics and the poor nutrition that results from poverty. He talks about 'curing' the community, not just through aid or charity, but through personal and familial responsibility for hygiene and nutrition. But he also recognizes the disparity between those who are a part of an ill-fed population existing next to those who live too luxuriously.[10] It becomes a social duty to look after one's individual body so that we remain useful, and also that we should seek to alleviate poverty where we can: self-care is not enough, but one must care for other members of the social body – 'The patience which endures removable evils is unacceptable'.[11] Lee concludes that if one cannot be persuaded to look after one's body, one will not be convinced to look after one's soul.[12] The onus of social health lies in individual health, but the willingness or otherwise to engage with healthy habits reveals the health of the nation's soul.

Self-moderation and the health of the nation

Many medical doctors throughout the nineteenth century persist in the metaphor of body as machine from a motive of creating a sense of scientific distance. The *Bridgewater Treatises* (1833–1840),[13] published specifically as a series to explicate natural theology, provide provocative examples of the engagement between medicine and theology in trying to understand the individual and social bodies, as well as how to keep those bodies healthy. For example, John Kidd emphasizes that he has been 'strictly called upon to consider, not the moral, but *the physical condition of man*',[14] while William Prout states that '[a] living being considered as an object of chemical research, is a laboratory, within which a number of chemical operations are conducted'.[15] Yet even within this distancing impetus, there is a recognition of a connection between body and soul that brings such distancing into question. Peter Mark Roget, although using the language of the animal body as a machine, asserts the power of feeling to challenge the extreme focus on the physical: 'But can this, which is mere physical existence, be the sole end of life? Is there no further purpose to be answered by structures so exquisitely contrived... ?'[16]

Within the *Bridgewater Treatises*, Prout is the most direct on the importance of food restraint or moderation. He writes:

> Providence has gifted man with reason; to his reason, therefore, is left the choice of his food and drink, and not to instinct, as among the lower animals: it thus becomes his duty to apply his reason to the regulation of his diet; to shun excess in quantity, and what is noxious in quality; to adhere, in short, to the simple and the natural; among which the bounty of his Maker has afforded him an ample selection; and beyond which if he deviates, sooner or later, he will suffer the penalty.[17]

Although he does not explicitly use the term 'fasting', Prout also goes on to discuss food abstinence as a natural and healthy part of human digestion:

> Many animals can and do live, for a considerable time, on substances contained in their own bodies. Thus, hibernating animals... have the ability to assimilate further, those matters which have already become a part of themselves; consequently, such a faculty of progressive organization as we have supposed, actually exists; and *a sort of digestion is carried on in all parts of the body, to fit for absorption and future appropriation, those matters which have been already assimilated.*[18]

The connection between health and food restraint that these doctors express is echoed in liturgical fasting. Within the theological context, ideas of the individual body's health, and how to manage that health, become extended to the health of the social body, by virtue of the emphasis on the Community of Saints and the Church as one body of many parts; that is, the Body of Christ. As in Rossetti's theology, the shift toward the Trinity as a model for the social body means that to care for the health and well-being for all members of that body is to show love for the divine. An incarnational theology of the social body requires a 'renewed vision of personhood' that is both material and spiritual,[19] expecting its adherents not just to recognize the divine in the Other in an abstract, spiritual sense, but actively work to realize their sacred equality in a material sense: their physical health and well-being, as well as access to social and economic agency. Fasting is meant to reinforce community connection and community aid, as well as an understanding of one's own position and responsibility within the social body. As a part of this idea of responsible fasting, it should not be practised to the extent of compromising one's own health and vitality, for to do so is detrimental not just to oneself, but to the social body. Importantly, ideas of national character, and therefore the health of the nation, are linked directly to the kind of self-government that fasting induces.

For the women addressed in this study, fasting was a complex practice that involved both spiritual and ethical conviction. For each of them, it had an outward purpose of direct and indirect social justice, which reworks the image of the faster cloistered away and diminishing physically and publicly. In fact, fasting was seen as a means to become more deeply connected to one another, rather than a means to separate oneself from the community. The fasting Body of Christ becomes a challenge to the Christian Church to do its duty in serving the community – feeding the hungry, clothing the naked – and also to the social body, that is, the broader British society, to address systemic inequalities in its institutions of power and authority. Within the broader context of the conversations between medicine and theology that developed throughout the century, moderated fasting enables the individual body to sustain its own strength and that of the nation. The health of the nation depends on the capacity of individuals to live actively in an attitude of interdependence, each individual's health determining, and being determined by, that of the social body.

Notes

1   Norman Porritt, *Religion and Health: Their Mutual Relationship and Influence* (London: Skeffington & Son, 1905), 1.

2   Catherine Gallagher, *The Body Economic: Life, Death, and Sensation in Political Economy and the Victorian Novel* (Princeton and Oxford: Princeton University Press, 2006), 22.
3   Pamela K. Gilbert, *Disease, Desire, and the Body in Victorian Women's Popular Novels* (Cambridge: Cambridge University Press, [1997] 2001), 1.
4   Emma-Jayne Abbots, *The Agency of Eating: Mediation, Food and the Body* (London: Bloomsbury, 2017), 3, 5.
5   Peter Jackson, *Anxious Appetites: Food and Consumer Culture* (London: Bloomsbury, 2015), 1.
6   Ibid., 8–9.
7   Robert Lee, *What Christianity Teaches Respecting the Body. A Sermon Preached in the Parish Church, Crathie, 11th October 1857* (Edinburgh: Cowan and Co.; Glasgow: Thomas Murray and Son; London: Houlston and Wright, 1857), 8.
8   Ibid., 14–15.
9   Ibid., 15, 17, 19.
10 Ibid., 21–2.
11 Ibid., 24.
12 Ibid., 30.
13 The *Bridgewater Treatises* were published almost in parallel to the Oxford Movement's *Tracts for the Times* and were commissioned in the will of the Earl of Bridgewater to reveal the glory of God through scientific discovery.
14 John Kidd, *On the Adaptation of External Nature to the Physical Condition of Man*. Bridgewater Treatises II (5th ed. London: William Pickering, 1837), 2. Emphasis orig.
15 William Prout, *Chemistry Meteorology and the Function of Digestion Considered with Reference to Natural Theology*. Bridgewater Treatises VIII (2nd ed. London: William Pickering, 1834), 417.
16 Peter Mark Roget, *Animal and Vegetable Physiology Considered with Reference to Natural Theology*. Bridgewater Treatises V. 2 vols. (3rd ed. London: William Pickering, 1840), 328.
17 Prout, *Chemistry Meteorology*, 514–15.

18 Ibid., 522. Emphasis orig.
19 Elizabeth Ludlow, *Christina Rossetti and the Bible: Waiting with the Saints* (London: Bloomsbury, 2014), 98.

Bibliography

Abbots, Emma-Jayne. *The Agency of Eating: Mediation, Food and the Body*. London: Bloomsbury, 2017.

Acton, Eliza. *The Elegant Economist*. 1845; London: Penguin, 2011.

Albala, Ken, ed. *Routledge International Handbook of Food Studies*. London and New York: Routledge, 2013.m k.

Arseneau, Mary. *Recovering Christina Rossetti: Female Community and Incarnational Poetics*. Hampshire: Palgrave, 2004.

Atkinson, Damian, ed. *The Selected Letters of Alice Meynell, Poet and Essayist*. Cambridge: Cambridge Scholars Publishing, 2013.

Badeni, June. *The Slender Tree: A Life of Alice Meynell*. Padstow, Cornwall: Tabb House, 1981.

Bamfield, Joshua. 'Consumer-Owned Community Flour and Bread Societies in the Eighteenth and Early Nineteenth Centuries', *Business History*, 40.4 (1998): 16–36.

Bauman, Zygmunt. *Does Ethics Have a Chance in a World of Consumers?* Institute for Human Sciences Vienna Lecture Series. Cambridge, MA and London: Harvard University Press, 2008.

Bell, Rudolph M. *Holy Anorexia*. Chicago: University of Chicago Press, 1985.

Blair, Kirstie. *Form and Faith in Victorian Poetry and Religion*. Oxford: Oxford University Press, 2012.

Blumberg, Ilana. *Victorian Sacrifice: Ethics and Economics in Mid-Century Novels*. Columbus: The Ohio State University Press, 2013.

Bowen, John. *The Russell Predictions on the Working Class, the National Debt, and the New Poor Law. Dissected*. London: Hatchard & Son, 1850.

Bowley, Mary. *Universal History on Scriptural Principles. Chiefly Designed for the Young*. London: Samuel Bagster and Sons, 1842.

Brumberg, Joan Jacobs. *Fasting Girls: The History of Anorexia Nervosa*. 1988; New York: Vintage Books, 2000.

Butler, Josephine. *An Autobiographical Memoir*, ed. George W. and Lucy A. Johnson. Bristol: J.W. Arrowsmith, 1909.

Butler, Josephine. *Catharine of Siena: A Biography*. 3rd ed. 1878; London: Horace Marshall & Son, 1894.

Butler, Josephine. *The Lady of Shunem*. London: Horace Marshall & Son, 1894.

Butler, Josephine. *Personal Reminiscences of a Great Crusade*. London: Horace Marshall and Son, 1910.

Butler, Josephine. *Prophets and Prophetesses: Some Thoughts for the Present Times*. London: Dyer Brothers, 1897.

Butler, Josephine, ed. *Woman's Work and Woman's Culture: A Series of Essays*. London: Macmillan, 1869.

Bynum, Caroline Walker. *Holy Feast and Holy Fast: The Religious Significance of Food to Medieval Women*. Berkeley: University of California Press, 1987.

Calvert, Samantha. 'A Taste of Eden: Modern Christianity and Vegetarianism', *Journal of Ecclesiastical History*, 58.3 (2007): 461–81.

Carruthers, Jo, Mark Knight and Andrew Tate, eds. *Literature and the Bible: A Reader*. London: Routledge, 2014.

Chalmers, Thomas. *On the Power Wisdom and Goodness of God as Manifested in the Adaptation of External Nature to the Moral and Intellectual Constitution of Man*. Bridgewater Treatises I. 2 vols. London: William Pickering, 1835.

Chambers, Robert, ed. *The Book of Days: A Miscellany of Popular Antiquities in Connection with the Calendar Including Anecdote, Biography, & History, Curiosities of Literature, and Oddities of Human Life and Character*. 2 vols. London and Edinburgh: W. & R. Chambers, 1869.

Chapple, J.A.V., ed. *Elizabeth Gaskell: A Portrait in Letters*. Manchester: Machester University Press, 1980.

Chapple, J.A.V. and Arthur Pollard, eds. *The Letters of Mrs Gaskell*. Manchester: Mandolin, 1997.

Cline, Sally. *Just Desserts: Women and Food*. London: Andre Deutsch Limited, 1990.

Coleridge, Samuel Taylor. '*Blessed are ye that sow beside all waters!*' *A Laysermon, Addressed to the Higher and Middle Classes, on the Existing Distresses and Discontents*. London: Gale and Fenner, 1817.

Colón, Susan E. *Victorian Parables*. London: Continuum, 2012.

Coveney, John. *Food, Morals and Meaning: The Pleasure and Anxiety of Eating*. London: Routledge, 2000.

Coveney, John. 'The Science and Spirituality of Nutrition', *Critical Public Health*, 9.1 (1999): 23–37.

Crane, Jonathan K. *Eating Ethically: Religion and Science for a Better Diet*. New York: Columbia University Press, 2018.

Craig, David. *John Ruskin and the Ethics of Consumption*. Charlottesville: University of Virginia Press 2006.

Crotty, Patricia. *Good Nutrition? Fact and Fashion in Dietary Advice*. St Leonard's: Allen and Unwin, 1995.

Cunningham, W. *The Growth of English Industry and Commerce in Modern Times*. Cambridge: Cambridge University Press, 1892.

Daggers, Jenny and Diana Neal, eds. *Sex, Gender, and Religion: Josephine Butler Revisited*. New York: Peter Lang, 2006.

Dalley, Lana and Jill Rappoport, eds. *Economic Women: Essays on Desire and Dispossession in Nineteenth-Century British Culture*. Columbus: The Ohio State University Press, 2013.

de Groot, Christiana and Marion Ann Taylor, eds. *Recovering Nineteenth-Century Women Interpreters of the Bible*. Leiden: Brill, 2007.

Dieleman, Karen. *Religious Imaginaries: The Liturgical and Poetic Practices of Elizabeth Barrett Browning, Christina Rossetti, and Adelaide Procter*. Athens: Ohio University Press, 2012.

Easson, Angus. *Elizabeth Gaskell*. London: Routledge and Kegan Paul, 1979.

Evans, Robert Wilson. *The Ministry of the Body*. London: Francis & John Rivington, 1847.

Farage, Amanda. '"Rhythm of Life, The" (Meynell)', in *The Palgrave Encyclopedia of Victorian Women's Writing*, ed. Lesa Scholl and Emily Morris. Palgrave Macmillan, 2021, https://doi.org/10.1007/978-3-030-02721-6_349-1.

Frye, Joshua J. and Michael S. Bruner, eds. *The Rhetoric of Food: Discourse, Materiality, and Power*. London: Routledge, 2012.

Gallagher, Catherine. *The Body Economic: Life, Death, and Sensation in Political Economy and the Victorian Novel*. Princeton and Oxford: Princeton University Press, 2006.

Gaskell, Elizabeth. *Cranford*. 1853; Oxford: Oxford University Press, 2011.

Gaskell, Elizabeth. *Mary Barton*. 1848; Oxford: Oxford University Press, 1998.

Gaskell, Elizabeth. *North and South*. 1854–5; London: Penguin, 1995.

Gaskell, Elizabeth. *Ruth*. 1853; London: Penguin, 1997.

Gilbert, Pamela. *Disease, Desire, and the Body in Victorian Women's Popular Novels*. 1997; Cambridge: Cambridge University Press, 2001.

Gilbert, Pamela. 'A Sinful and Suffering Nation: Cholera and the Evolution of Medical and Religious Authority in Britain, 1832–1866', *Nineteenth-Century Prose*, 25.1 (1998): 26–45.

Gleadle, Kathryn. *Borderline Citizens: Women, Gender, and Political Culture in Britain 1815–1867*. Oxford: Oxford University Press, 2009.

Goodman, Michael K., Damian Maye and Lewis Holloway. 'Ethical Foodscapes?: Premises, Promises, and Possibilities', *Environment and Planning*, 42 (2010): 1782–96.

Gray, F. Elizabeth, ed. *Women in Journalism at the* Fin de Siècle: *Making a Name for Herself*. Basingstoke: Palgrave, 2012.

Gregory, James. *Of Victorians and Vegetarians: The Vegetarian Movement in Nineteenth-Century Britain*. London: Tauris Academic Studies, 2007.

Griffin, Ben. *The Politics of Gender in Victorian Britain: Masculinity, Political Culture and the Struggle for Women's Rights*. Cambridge: Cambridge University Press, 2012.

Halévy, Élie. *The Triumph of Reform: 1830–1841*, trans. E. I. Watkin. New York: Barns & Noble, 1961.

Hargrove, James L. 'History of the Calorie in Nutrition', *The Journal of Nutrition*, 136.12 (2006): 2957–61.

Heise, Ursula K., Jon Christensen and Michelle Niemann, eds. *The Routledge Companion to the Environmental Humanities*. New York and London: Routledge, 2017.

Heywood, Leslie. *Dedication to Hunger: The Anorexic Aesthetic in Modern Culture*. Berkeley: University of California Press, 1996.

Holland, Henry. *Medical Notes and Reflections*. London: Longman, Orme, Brown, Green, and Longmans, 1839.

Horne, Thomas A. '"The Poor Have a Claim Founded in the Law of Nature": William Paley and the Rights of the Poor', *Journal of the History of Philosophy*, 23.1 (1985): 51–70.

Houston, Gail Turley. *Consuming Fictions: Gender, Class, and Hunger in Dickens's Novels*. Carbondale: Southern Illinois University Press, 1994.

Ismay, Penelope. *Trust among Strangers: Friendly Societies in Modern Britain*. Cambridge: Cambridge University Press, 2018.

Jackson, Peter. *Anxious Appetites: Food and Consumer Culture*. London: Bloomsbury, 2015.

Jantzen, Grace M. *Power, Gender and Christian Mysticism*. Cambridge: Cambridge University Press, 1995.

Jordan, Jane. *Josephine Butler*. 2001; London: Hambledon Continuum, 2007.

Kamminga, Harmke and Andrew Cunningham, eds. *The Science and Culture of Nutrition, 1840–1940*. Amsterdam: Rodopi, 1995.

Kidd, John. *On the Adaptation of External Nature to the Physical Condition of Man*. Bridgewater Treatises II. 5th ed. London: William Pickering, 1837.

King, Joshua. *Imagined Spiritual Communities in Britain's Age of Print*. Columbus: Ohio State University Press, 2015.

King, Joshua and Winter Jade Werner, eds. *Constructing Nineteenth-Century Religion: Literary, Historical, and Religious Studies in Dialogue*. Columbus: Ohio State University Press, 2019.

Knight, Mark. *An Introduction to Religion and Literature*. London: Continuum, 2009.

Korsmeyer, Carolyn. *Making Sense of Taste: Food and Philosophy*. Ithaca: Cornell University Press, 1999.

Laas, Molly. *Nutrition as a Social Question 1835–1905*. University of Wisconsin-Maddison, PhD Dissertation, History of Science, Medicine, and Technology, 2017.

Larson, Janet L. 'Josephine Butler's *Catharine of Siena*: Writing (Auto) Biography as a Feminist Spiritual Practice', *Christianity and Literature*, 48.4 (1999): 445–71.

Larson, Janet L. 'Praying Bodies, Spectacular Martyrs, and the Virile Sisterhood: "Salutary and Useful Confusions" in Josephine Butler's *Catharine of Siena*', *Christianity and Literature*, 49.1 (1999): 3–34.

Lee, Robert. *What Christianity Teaches Respecting the Body. A Sermon Preached in the Parish Church, Crathie, 11th October 1857*. Edinburgh: Cowan and Co.; Glasgow: Thomas Murray and Son; London: Houlston and Wright, 1857.

Levinas, Emmanuel. *Otherwise than Being or Beyond Essence*, trans. Alphonso Lingis. 1981; Pittsburgh: Duquesne University Press, 1998.

Lewis, Tania and Emily Potter, eds. *Ethical Consumption: A Critical Introduction*. London and New York: Routledge, 2010.

Logan, Trevon D. 'Food, Nutrition, and Substitution in the Late Nineteenth Century', *Explorations in Economic History*, 43 (2006): 527–45.

Ludlow, Elizabeth. *Christina Rossetti and the Bible: Waiting with the Saints*. London: Bloomsbury, 2014.

Mason, Emma. 'Christina Rossetti and the Doctrine of Reserve', *Journal of Victorian Culture*, 7.2 (2002): 196–219.

Mason, Emma. *Christina Rossetti: Poetry, Ecology, Faith*. Oxford: Oxford University Press, 2018.

Mason, Emma, ed. *Reading the Abrahamic Faiths: Rethinking Religion and Literature*. London: Bloomsbury, 2015.

Mathers, Helen. 'The Evangelical Spirituality of a Victorian Feminist: Josephine Butler, 1828–1906', *Journal of Ecclesiastical History*, 52.2 (2001): 282–312.

Matsuoka, Mitsuharu, ed. *Evil and its Variations in the Works of Elizabeth Gaskell: Sesquicentennial Essays*. Osaka: Osaka Kyoiku Tosho, 2015.

McCloskey, Deirdre N. *The Bourgeois Virtues: Ethics for an Age of Commerce*. Chicago: University of Chicago Press, 2006.

McCollum, Elmer Verner. *A History of Nutrition: The Sequence of Ideas in Nutrition Investigations*. Boston: Houghton Mifflin Company, 1957.

Melnyk, Julie, ed. *Women's Theology in Nineteenth-Century Britain: Transfiguring the Faith of Their Fathers*. New York: Garland Publishing, 1998.

Meynell, Alice. *Ceres' Runaway & Other Essays*. New York: John Lane, 1910.

Meynell, Alice. *Poems*. London: Burns & Oates, 1913.

Meynell, Alice. *The Poor Sisters of Nazareth: An Illustrated Record of Life at Nazareth House, Hammersmith*. 1889; New Delhi: Isha Books, 2013.

Meynell, Alice. *The Rhythm of Life & Other Essays*. London and New York: John Lane, 1905.

Meynell, Viola. *Alice Meynell: A Memoir*. London: Jonathan Cape, 1929.

Moleschott, Jacob. *The Chemistry of Food and Diet: With a Chapter on Food Adulterations. Including Constituents of the Human Body, Digestive and*

Secretive Organs, and the Physiological Principles of Diet, trans. Edward Bronner and John Scoffern. London: Houlston and Stoneman, 1856.

Moore, George. *The Power of the Soul over the Body, Considered in Relation to Health and Morals*. 1845; New York: Harper & Brothers, 1847.

Moore, Jason W. *Capitalism in the Web of Life: Ecology and the Accumulation of Capital*. London: Verso, 2015.

Morrison, Kevin A. *Victorian Liberalism and Material Culture: Synergies of Thought and Place*. Edinburgh: Edinburgh University Press, 2019.

Newman, Lucile F., ed. *Hunger in History: Food Shortage, Poverty, and Deprivation*. 1990; Oxford: Blackwell Publishers, 1995.

Nichols, Thomas Low. *The Diet Cure: An Essay on the Relations of Food and Drink, Health, Disease and Cure*. New York: M.L. Holbrook and Co., 1881.

Nichols, Thomas Low. *How to Live on a Dime and a-Half a-Day*. New York: J.S. Redfield, 1872.

Nunokawa, Jeff. *The Afterlife of Property: Domestic Security and the Victorian Novel*. Princeton: Princeton University Press, 1994.

Obelkevich, Jim, Lyndal Roper and Raphael Samuel, eds. *Disciplines of Faith: Studies in Religion, Politics and Patriarchy*. London: Routledge, 1987.

Ó Gráda, Cormac. *Famine: A Short History*. Princeton: Princeton University Press, 2009.

Otter, Christopher. *Diet for a Large Planet: Industrial Britain, Food Systems, and World Ecology*. Chicago: University of Chicago Press, 2020.

Packham, Catherine. 'The Physiology of Political Economy: Vitalism and Adam Smith's *Wealth of Nations*', *Journal of the History of Ideas*, 63.3 (2002): 465–81.

Palazzo, Lynda. *Christina Rossetti's Feminist Theology*. Hampshire: Palgrave, 2002.

Paley, William. *The Principles of Moral and Political Philosophy*. 1785; 5th ed. Dublin: Byrne, McKenzie and Jones, 1893.

Patrick, Simon. *A Treatise of Repentance and Fasting*, ed. F. E. Paget. Oxford: J.H. Parker, 1841.

Pilcher, Jeffrey M., ed. *The Oxford Handbook of Food History*. 2012; Oxford: Oxford University Press, 2017.

Pionke, Albert D. *Plots of Opportunity: Representing Conspiracy in Victorian England*. Columbus: Ohio State University Press, 2004.

Poovey, Mary. *Making a Social Body: British Cultural Formation 1830–1864*. Chicago and London: University of Chicago Press, 1995.

Porritt, Norman. *Religion and Health: Their Mutual Relationship and Influence*. London: Skeffington & Son, 1905.

Poynter, J. R. *Society and Pauperism: English Ideas on Poor Relief, 1795–1834*. Toronto: University of Toronto Press, 1969.

Pratt, John Tidd, ed. *The Law of Friendly Societies and industrial and provident societies: with the acts, observations thereon, forms of rules, etc., reports of leading cases at length, and a copious index*. London: Shaw, 1909.

Pritchard, Bill, Rodomiro Ortiz and Meera Shekar, eds. *The Routledge Handbook on Food and Nutrition Security*. London: Routledge, 2016.

Prout, William. *Chemistry Meteorology and the Function of Digestion Considered with Reference to Natural Theology*. Bridgewater Treatises VIII. 2nd ed. London: William Pickering, 1834.

Rappoport, Jill. *Giving Women: Alliance and Exchange in Victorian Culture*. Oxford: Oxford University Press, 2012.

Rich, Rachel. *Bourgeois Consumption: Food, Space and Identity in London and Paris, 1850–1914*. Manchester: Manchester University Press, 2011.

[Robinson, Nicholas]. *A treatise on the virtues and efficacy of a crust of bread, eat early in a morning fasting: to which are added, some particular remarks concerning cures accomplished by the saliva... with some critical observations concerning the recrements of the blood... by a physician*. London: Burgess and Hill, 1821.

Roget, Peter Mark. *Animal and Vegetable Physiology Considered with Reference to Natural Theology*. Bridgewater Treatises V. 2 vols. 3rd ed. London: William Pickering, 1840.

Rossetti, Christina G. *The Face of the Deep: A Devotional Commentary on the Apocalypse*. 2nd ed. London: SPCK, 1893.

Rossetti, Christina G. *Letter and Spirit. Notes on the Commandments*. Published under the Direction of the Tract Committee. Oxford: Clarendon Press, 1883.

Rossetti, Christina G. *The Letters of Christina Rossetti*, ed. Antony H. Harrison. 4 vols; Charlottesville: University Press of Virginia, 1997.

Rossetti, Christina G. *Seek and Find: A Double Series of Short Studies of the Benedicite*. London: SPCK, 1879.

Rossetti, Christina G. *Time Flies: A Reading Diary*. 1886; London: SPCK, 1901.

Rowell, Geoffrey. *The Vision Glorious: Themes and Personalities of the Catholic Revival in Anglicanism*. Oxford: Oxford University Press, 1991.

Schmemann, Alexander. *Introduction to Liturgical Theology*. Crestwood, NY: St Vladimir's Seminary Press, 1966.

Scholl, Lesa. *Hunger, Poetry and the Oxford Movement: The Tractarian Social Vision*. London: Bloomsbury, 2020.

Sen, Amartya. *Poverty and Famines: An Essay on Entitlement and Deprivation*. Oxford: Oxford University Press, 1981.

Shakespeare, William. *The Merchant of Venice*. 1596–97; London: Penguin, 1965.

Silver, Anna Krugovoy. *Victorian Literature and the Anorexic Body*. Cambridge: Cambridge University Press, 2002.

Spencer, Rev. Thomas. *Objections to the New Poor Law Answered, Part 4*. London: John Green, 1841.

Styler, Rebecca. 'Josephine Butler's Serial Auto/Biography: Writing the Changing Self through the Lives of Others', *Life Writing*, 14.2 (2017): 171–84.

Styler, Rebecca. *Literary Theology by Women Writers of the Nineteenth Century*. Farnham: Ashgate, 2010.

Taylor, Jeremy. *The Whole Works of the Right Rev. Jeremy Taylor, D. D*, ed. Reginald Heber. vol. 4. London: Ogle, Duncan and Co., 1822.

Thompson, E. P. *The Making of the English Working Class*. New York: Vintage, 1966.

[Todd, Robert Bentley]. *Remarks on Fasting, and on the Discipline of the Body: In a Letter to a Clergyman. By A Physician*. London: Francis & John Rivington, 1848.

Torrington, F. William, ed. *House of Lords Sessional Papers*. Session 1799–1800. 2 vols. New York: Oceana Publication, 1975.

Tusan, Michelle. *Smyrna's Ashes: Humanitarianism, Genocide, and the Birth of the Middle East*. Berkeley: University of California Press, 2012.

Tynan, Katharine. 'Mrs. Meynell and Her Poetry', *Catholic World*, 97 (1913): 668–76.

Vernon, James. *Hunger: A Modern History*. Cambridge, MA: Belknap Press, 2007.

Wagner, Corinna. *Pathological Bodies: Medicine and Political Culture*. Berkeley: University of California Press, 2013.

Wagner, Tamara S. and Narin Hassan, eds. *Consuming Culture in the Long Nineteenth Century: Narratives of Consumption, 1700–1900*. Lanham: Lexington Books, 2007.

Walton, Heather, ed. *Literature and Theology: New Interdisciplinary Spaces*. London and New York: Routledge, 2011.

Webb, Sidney and Beatrice Webb. 'The Assize of Bread', *The Economic Journal*, 14.54 (June 1904): 196–218.

Weiner, Annette B. *Inalienable Possessions: The Paradox of Keeping-While-Giving*. Berkeley: University of California Press, 1992.

Williams, Todd O. 'The Autobiographical Self and Embodied Knowledge of God in Christina Rossetti's *Time Flies*', *Literature & Theology*, 28.3 (2014): 321–33.

Wirzba, Norman. *Food and Faith: A Theology of Eating*. 2nd ed. Cambridge: Cambridge University Press, 2019.

Wirzba, Norman. *From Nature to Creation: A Christian Vision for Understanding and Loving Our World*. Grand Rapids, MI: Baker Academic, 2015.

Wohl, Anthony S. *Endangered Lives: Public Health in Victorian Britain*. London: Methuen, 1983.

Woolfenden, Graham. 'Eastern Christian Liturgical Traditions: Eastern Orthodox', in *The Blackwell Companion to Eastern Christianity*, ed. Ken Parry. 319–38. London: Blackwell, 2007.

Young, Arthur, ed. *Annals of Agriculture, and Other Useful Arts*. Vol 36. London: Richardson, 1801.

Index

abolition 30, 84–5
abstinence 7, 11–12, 17, 25–6, 38, 51–2, 91, 100, 113–14, 123, 128, 137
agency 1, 11–13, 16, 37, 41–2, 91–2, 98, 103, 118–20, 125, 134
  economic 1, 16, 28, 32, 138
  moral 39
  social 1, 16, 31–2, 37, 92, 138
Anglican and Eastern Orthodox Churches Union 50
Anglicanism 8–15, 18–19, 47–50, 56, 64, 67, 77, 80, 85, 113, 127, 130
  High Anglicanism 52, 54, 59, 119
Anglo-Catholicism *See also* High Anglicanism 8–9, 80, 127
Ankeny, Rachel 2
anorexia 8–15, 90–1
  anorexia mirabilis 11–12
  anorexia nervosa 2, 11–12, 15, 91–2, 116
  anorexic space 89–97
Anti-Saccharite Movement 29
apocalypse 68, 88–9, 100
appetite 1, 40, 51–2, 56, 62–3, 72, 90, 116, 117–18, 134
Arseneau, Mary 48
asceticism 12, 47–8, 93, 95, 97
Augustine 10

Badeni, June 113, 115, 116, 117
biography *See also* life-writing 78–80, 82, 90, 92, 93, 113
Blair, Kirstie 48
blood 111–12, 121, 123
Blumberg, Ilana 26
Body of Christ 17–18, 43, 48, 49, 51, 54, 55–9, 60, 66, 67, 72, 111, 112, 122–3, 126, 133–8

Bridgewater Treatises 136, 139 n. 13
Broad Church 18, 81
Butler, Josephine 8, 17, 18, 26, 77–104, 133

calories 110–11
Capitalism 3, 4, 10, 12, 32, 68, 82, 96, 97, 98–101
Catharine of Siena 78, 89–98
Catharine of Siena (Butler) 89–98
charity 13, 18, 42, 52, 67, 69, 72, 91, 112, 127, 128–9, 135
Christianity 48, 50, 77, 135
Christian Socialism 18, 81, 112, 127
Church of England *See also* Anglicanism 25, 50
collective responsibility 5
commodities 6, 16, 29, 31, 72
common feeling *See also* fellow-feeling 33, 37, 40, 41, 43
communion of the saints 56, 64, 137
community 2, 5–8, 10, 12, 13, 17, 23, 24, 26, 33–4, 35, 37, 38, 40, 47, 48, 54–5, 56, 63–4, 66, 71–2, 85, 96, 123, 126, 127, 128, 133, 134, 135, 138
Consumerism 2, 4, 5, 10, 15, 29, 31, 49, 53, 68, 98, 128, 134
Contagious Diseases Acts 79
cooperative movements 5
Corn Laws, the 30–1
Coveney, John 12, 109–10
Cranford (Gaskell) 25, 33–7, 38, 41, 43

Dalley, Lana 6, 23, 24, 91
diet 4, 14, 16, 17, 29, 31, 35, 70, 90, 91, 95, 110, 111–12, 116–18, 137

dietary abstinence 7, 12, 25–33, 91, 95
dietary reform 7
dietary restraint 113–18
dietary restriction societies 5, 85
diplomacy 36–8, 41–2
divine unity 56

Eastern Orthodoxy 12, 49–51, 52, 56, 59–60, 65, 67, 113
ecology 4, 10
economics 1, 3–7, 16, 23–43, 67, 69–72, 84–7, 91, 97, 98, 101, 129, 135, 138
   economic crisis 26
   economic privilege 16, 25, 27–8, 31
   economic vulnerability/precarity 7, 27, 39, 41–3, 79
   and ethics 23–43
   moral economy 3, 24, 26, 85–6, 91
   political economy 4, 5, 23–4, 25, 69, 72, 128
Economic Women (Dalley and Rappoport) 6, 23
Ecumenism 25, 26, 94
empathy 17, 25–33, 57, 73, 103, 114, 126
Esau 62–3, 66
ethical choice 25, 91–2
ethical consumption 2–3, 12
Eucharist 8, 54, 111–12, 121–4, 128, 132 n. 35
Evangelicalism 67, 80–1, 85
Evans, Robert Wilson 13–14, 21 n. 35, 47–8, 57, 66, 73
excess 4, 10, 11, 12–13, 14–16, 19, 27, 28, 34–7, 53, 54–5, 57, 59, 60, 62–3, 68, 70–1, 73, 88, 90, 92, 96, 98, 120, 121, 125, 126, 129, 137
   culture of 92

Face of the Deep, The (Rossetti) 57, 60–1, 63–4, 68
famine 4, 62, 63–4

Farage, Amanda 120
fasting 6, 10–15, 16–17, 43, 47–8, 51–2, 57, 59, 60–4, 71, 72–3, 78–9, 98, 100, 103, 112–14, 116, 118, 123, 126, 128, 130, 133, 137–8
   corporate 63
   ethics of 53–5, 66–7, 95, 127
   extreme 10–11, 13, 90–1
   liturgical 1, 8, 10, 63, 65–7, 114, 118–19, 121, 137
   regulation of 8, 14–15, 17, 121
fasting girls 11, 17, 91
fellow-feeling 17, 43, 54, 56
Flammang, Lucretia 83, 84
food 1–2, 6, 15–16, 19, 24, 29–31, 35–6, 37, 39, 40, 42, 52–3, 58–9, 62, 64, 67, 71, 84–6, 89, 90–2, 96, 98, 100, 112–13, 135
   access 1, 43
   choices 2, 16, 39, 110
   consumption of 1, 2, 3, 16, 26, 29, 52, 109, 116, 134
   ethics 2, 4, 6, 28, 109–10
   exchange 26, 42
   practices 1
   refusal 11, 13
   restraint 2, 4, 6, 8, 11, 12–13, 15, 16, 17–18, 28, 43, 52, 91–2, 95–6, 123, 127–30, 133, 136–7
   waste 63–4, 85–6, 117, 129
foodscapes 3–4, 28, 31

Gagnier, Regenia 27
Gallagher, Catherine 134
Gaskell, Elizabeth 8, 17, 18, 23–43, 78, 81, 103, 130–1 n. 11, 133
Gilbert, Pamela 134
Gleadle, Kathryn 5, 7, 26, 85, 91
gluttony 10, 14–15, 19, 53, 55–6, 57, 59, 62–3, 71–3, 85, 98–102

hagiography 17, 18, 77–104, 113
health 2, 14–17, 29, 48, 51–2, 55–6, 57, 59, 61, 71, 72–3, 87, 95, 98–9, 109–10, 112–13, 116–19, 133–8

Hopkins, Gerard Manley 12
hospitality 32–6, 38–43, 82, 101–2, 109, 115–16

imperialism 4, 29, 49, 59, 61, 67, 110
industrialization 5, 6, 7, 9, 42, 67, 98, 134

Jordan, Jane 80, 83–4

Kidd, John 136
Korsmeyer, Carolyn 39–40

Lady of Shunem, The (Butler) 101–2
Larson, Janet 78, 90–1, 96
Lee, Robert 135–6
Lent 65
Letter and Spirit (Rossetti) 53–4, 55–7, 61–3, 68
Levinas, Emmanuel 16, 98
life-writing 78
liturgy 10, 12, 48, 50–1, 54, 59–67, 69–70, 77, 114, 118, 120–2, 137
Ludlow, Elizabeth 8, 18, 25–6, 48–9, 130–1 n. 11
luxury 10, 28, 29–31, 35, 38, 53, 57, 59, 62, 68–9, 72, 109, 117, 128, 135

Mary Barton (Gaskell) 25, 34, 46 n. 41
Mason, Emma 8, 9, 48, 49
Materialist Theology 17, 48–55, 72
Mathers, Helen 77, 80
Maurice, F. D. 18, 81
medicine 11, 14, 19, 21 n. 35, 51, 73, 112, 118, 133–4, 135, 136, 138
Methodism 25–6
Meynell, Alice 8, 17–18, 81, 109–30, 133
Millennialism 18, 25–6
Ministry of the Body, The (Evans) 13–14, 47–8
moderation 4, 10, 14, 15–17, 19, 39, 48, 49, 59, 62, 64, 66, 67, 69–70, 97, 117, 126, 130, 136–7, 138
Moleschott, Jacob 111–12, 121

Moore, George 51–2
moral health 87, 99

nature 2, 4, 8–10, 24, 47, 52–3, 56, 57–8, 111–12, 116, 135
Neale, John Mason 49, 50
necessity 29, 31, 35, 62, 67, 96
New Poor Law 5, 6–7, 23–4
Newman, John Henry 12, 13–14, 127
Nichols, Thomas Low 116–18, 121
North and South (Gaskell) 35, 37–9, 41–2, 43
nourishment 24, 55, 57, 86, 111–12, 117–18
  spiritual 66
nutrition 4, 12–13, 16, 109–10, 112, 116–18, 121, 135

obesity 2, 19
orthorexia 1
Otherwise than Being (Levinas) 16, 98
Oxford Movement, The 8, 12, 13, 47, 48–50, 119, 127, 139 n. 13

Palazzo, Lynda 48
Paley, William 85
physical strength 95, 113, 118, 130
physiology 110–11, 134
Plymley, Jane 12–13, 80, 91
Plymley, Joseph 5, 7, 21 n. 35, 80, 85–6
Plymley, Katherine 5, 7, 80, 85–6, 91
poetry 48–9, 51, 54, 112, 115, 119–26
  poetic restraint 48
Poor Sisters of Nazareth, The (Meynell) 127–30
poverty 4, 5–6, 15–16, 31–4, 38, 43, 58, 59, 69, 72, 32–4, 97, 103, 114, 115, 125–6, 128, 135–6
Poverty and Famines (Sen) 6
Practical Theology 8, 18, 25, 26, 78
privilege 6, 7, 12, 16, 19, 25, 27, 28, 29, 30–1, 35, 42, 55, 64, 66, 72, 86–9, 96, 97–8, 99, 101, 103, 126
Prophets and Prophetesses (Butler) 77, 98

Prout, William 136–7
public health 51, 112, 134, 135–6
Pusey, Edward Bouverie 10–11, 14, 15, 16–17, 48, 49, 50

Rappoport, Jill 6, 23, 24, 91, 127
rational thought 12–13, 15, 25, 92, 95, 102, 109, 127
Remarks on Fasting (Todd) 1, 14–15, 118
Rivington's Theological Library 47
Roman Catholicism 11–12, 14, 47, 49–50, 56, 65, 103, 112, 113, 116, 119, 126, 127
  emancipation of 50
Romanism *See also* Roman Catholicism 47
Rossetti, Christina 8, 9, 17, 18, 26, 43, 47–73, 77, 78, 80, 99, 104 n. 2, 133, 137
Ruth (Gaskell) 27–33, 35, 39, 40, 41, 43, 103
'Rhythm of Life, The' (Meynell) 120

sacramental 56, 60, 132 n. 35
saints 11, 49, 54, 56, 64, 65, 77–85, 89–98, 103–4, 121, 137
scarcity 4, 55, 63–4
Schmemann, Alexander 59
Seek and Find (Rossetti) 55, 58–9
self-restraint 85
Sen, Amartya 6, 16, 42
senses 1, 14, 36, 39–40, 51–3, 62, 117, 123–6, 134
Shelley, Percy Bysshe 29–30, 119
social action 10, 13, 24, 79, 92, 95, 97, 112
social body 13, 34, 43, 55, 56, 59, 72–3, 126, 133–8
social justice 7, 8, 12, 15, 18, 26, 31, 48, 49, 51, 54–5, 61, 68, 77, 78, 79, 80, 83, 98, 103, 112, 123, 126, 138
social prophecy 10, 17, 66–73, 77, 80–1, 88, 98
social transformation 78, 126

social welfare 23
spiritual growth 10, 13, 51, 53, 127
starvation 6, 12, 13, 14–15, 17, 19, 26, 35, 42–3, 59, 62, 64, 83–4, 88–9, 90–2, 126
Styler, Rebecca 78, 100
Sugar Boycott *See also* Anti-Saccharite Movement 7
Sugar Duties Act 30–1
sustenance 1, 40, 73, 86–7, 116, 129

temporality 18, 56, 62–3, 68
theology 4, 8–9, 11, 17–19, 25–6, 43, 47, 48–55, 57, 59–62, 65–7, 69–70, 72, 73, 77–80, 81–4, 86, 87–8, 94, 96, 98, 99, 100, 104, 111, 112–13, 118, 119–26, 133, 134, 135, 136, 137–8
Thompson, E. P. 5
Thoughts on the Benefits of the System of Fasting (Pusey) 10–11
Times Flies (Rossetti) 65–6
Todd, Robert Bentley 1, 13–14, 118, 121
'To the Body' (Meynell) 123–6
Tracts for the Times 10, 14, 139 n. 13
Tractarianism *See also* the Oxford Movement 8–9, 47, 48–9, 69
trade unions 5
Tusan, Michelle 50
Tynan, Katharine 109, 115

Unitarianism 18, 25–6
'Unknown God, The' (Meynell) 121–3

veganism 2
vegetarianism 2, 114, 116–17
Verses (Rossetti) 65, 72

Wagner, Corinna 29, 30
waste 4, 15, 32, 34, 35–6, 39, 59, 64, 69–71, 85, 86–7, 88, 96, 129
Woman's Work and Woman's Culture (Butler) 77–8, 86–9, 96
workhouses 24, 103

www.ingramcontent.com/pod-product-compliance
Lightning Source LLC
Chambersburg PA
CBHW061841300426
44115CB00013B/2464